Functional Phonetics Workbook

Functional Phonetics Workbook

Mary Lou Marsoun Cancio, M.A., CCC-SLP
Sadanand Singh, Ph.D.

PLURAL
PUBLISHING
INC.

SAN DIEGO
OXFORD
BRISBANE

5521 Ruffin Road
San Diego, CA 92123

e-mail: info@pluralpublishing.com
Web site: http://www.pluralpublishing.com

49 Bath Street
Abingdon, Oxfordshire OX14 1EA
United Kingdom

FSC
Mixed Sources
Product group from well-managed
forests and other controlled sources

Cert no. SW-COC-002283
www.fsc.org
© 1996 Forest Stewardship Council

Typeset in 11/14 Stone Informal by Flanagan's Publishing Services, Inc.
Printed in the United States of America by McNaughton and Gunn, Inc.
2nd printing, September 2009

ISBN-13: 978-1-59756-094-8
ISBN-10: 1-59756-094-4

Library of Congress Cataloging-in-Publication Data

Contents

Preface

The *Functional Phonetics Workbook* was designed to be used in several ways. It is a valuable classroom resource for instructors who teach an introductory phonetics course. In addition it can be used, along with the accompanying audio CDs, for individuals to learn the International Phonetic Alphabet (IPA) who may not have access to formal instruction. The Workbook also serves as a convenient review format for those who require a "brush-up" on their phonetic transcription skills.

The Workbook focuses on the basics of phonetic transcription in Standard American English, which makes it a very valuable resource for individuals who are English language learners. Students should find the Flash Cards a helpful study tool for learning the sound-IPA symbol association.

Having taught an introductory phonetics course for over 10 years has refined my view of the basics required for students learning phonetics and becoming competent transcribers. Seeing the success of hundreds of my students as they become phoneticians has brought great satisfaction.

I wish you the same success.

Mary Lou Marsoun Cancio,
M.A., CCC-SLP

Acknowledgments

Centuries ago, I was a student in Dr. Thayne Hedge's Introductory Phonetics class. He lives on in my memories as a wonderful instructor of my favorite subject. I thank Dr. Giri Hegde for his gentle prodding, encouragement, and suggestions. I am honored that Dr. S. Singh saw the potential of the coursebook and agreed to serve as co-author. The help of Lauren Duffy and Sandy Doyle of Plural Publishing during the preparation of the Workbook is very much appreciated.

Without the computer expertise of Pamela Wing, the Workbook would not have been completed. Her helpful suggestions, patience, and sweet nature were invaluable. Cheryl Andrews deserves credit for originating the phoneme page format.

The voices you hear on the audio CDs belong to Taylor Harris, Kimberly Lenz, Andrew Sessions, and Scott Calderwood. They were all students in my Spring, 2006 Phonetics class and agreed to devote their time to recording the transcription exercises. Thanks also to Kevin Wing who provided his vocal talents for the CDs. You guys are awesome!

Ray Settle of Maximus Studios in Fresno, California was a great help in organizing the CD recording schedule. Eric Sherbon, engineer extraordinaire, is responsible for the accuracy of the exercises and making the recording process fun. Ericka Olsen, Kim Bettencourt, and Pamela Wing agreed to listen to the CDs to ensure interlistener reliability of the transcription exercise answers. My gratitude to them!

To the Marsoun Clan and my friends for their support—you are a blessing in my life.

Mary Lou Marsoun Cancio

Workbook Format

In the order found in the Workbook, an exercise to determine initial-medial-final position of a phoneme is provided, including the transcription exercise number and corresponding track on the audio CDs. Each track is also identified by the CD number (1 or 2). A phonetic transcription exercise follows, with a reference to the Phoneme Study Card and track on the audio CDs.

A phoneme description page is provided for IPA phonemes. Each page is organized to provide the following information (see example on next page): (1) description of place and manner and listing of distinctive features, (2) vocal fold and velopharyngeal port position, (3) tongue position and how the phoneme is produced, (4) variations in spelling, (5) word position in Standard American English (SAE), and (6) clinical information. The Clinical Information section includes a listing of a consonant cognate (sound made in the same place and the same manner), common articulatory substitutions (replacement of one phoneme for another), or omission (absence of a phoneme and another phoneme does not replace it).

A Crossword Puzzle and Word Search are also included and provide more practice in phonetic transcription. Answers to all of the Crossword Puzzles and Word Searches are listed in Appendix B: Answers to Exercises.

Example of the Phoneme Description Page

Distinctive Features	Tongue Position
1.	3.
Voicing/Velopharyngeal Port	**Spelling Variations**
2.	4.
Word Position	**Clinical Information**
5.	6.

The International Phonetic Alphabet (IPA)

The English have no respect for their language, and will not teach their children to speak it. They cannot spell it because they have nothing to spell it with but an old foreign alphabet of which only the consonants—and not all of them—have any agreed speech value. Consequently no man can teach himself what it should sound like from reading it . . .

George Bernard Shaw, Preface to *Pygmalion*

As George Bernard Shaw laments, the "old foreign alphabet" does not provide a reliable sound-symbol representation of speech sounds.

In 1886, the International Phonetic Association developed a sound-symbol system based on an earlier alphabet developed by British phonetician Henry Sweet. This system was to be used to represent the sounds of all the languages of the world and allowed phoneticians a system to communicate with each other.

If our spoken speech could be accurately represented by the English alphabet, then we would have no need for a phonetic alphabet. Let's take a brief look at how we spell and pronounce some common English words. Although we have only some 40 sounds in English, we have more than 200 ways of spelling them using our alphabet. For example, the sound of "sh" has up to 14 different spellings (faction, shoot, sugar, mis-

sion, ocean, champagne, etc.), the long "o" sound can be represented by over a dozen spellings (crow, so, doe, beau, etc.), and the long "a" sound in our alphabet is represented by 12 different spellings (lay, take, maid, freight, great, hey, etc.). Many consonants also are represented in several different ways. Consider the spelling of "t" in thank, tender, notion, the "h" in ache, hoist, hour, three, and enough, and the "c" in chair, bloc, and citrus. Although there has been a constant push from various groups to regularize our spelling, these movements have been met with resistance for centuries. You can see that mastery of the phonetic alphabet is an absolute necessity for anyone who needs an unambiguous, one-to-one representation of spoken speech. The phonetic alphabet meets this need.

Phonetic symbols are placed in slash marks or virgules such as /k/. Brackets [ ] are used to indicate a group of connected speech sounds.

Many consonant symbols of the IPA originate from the Roman alphabet: p, b, t, d, k, g, l, m, n, r, f, v, s, z, and w. Other symbols are from the Greek alphabet or have been created especially for the IPA. The "x" is not found in the IPA and is represented by /ks/, as "q" is represented by /kw/. Similarly, the "c" is represented by a /k/ in words with a "k" sound.

The Greek capital Theta /θ/ is used for the voiceless "th" as in "**th**igh." The /ð/ represents the voiced "th" as in "**th**is." An upside down "w" /ʍ/ or /hw/ is used for the voiceless "wh" as in "**wh**eat."

A lengthened sigmoid /ʃ/ represents the "sh" as in "**sh**ip." The /ʒ/ symbolizes the "zh" sound as in "bei**ge**." The IPA combines the symbols /t/ and /ʃ/ into /tʃ/ for the "ch" sound as in "**ch**ick." Similarly, the /d/ and /ʒ/ join for /dʒ/ as in "**J**ack." The symbol /ŋ/ represents the "ng" sound as in "ri**ng**." The /j/ may look familiar to you, but in the IPA it is used to represent the "y" sound as in "**y**oung." IPA symbols for English consonants are shown in Table 1–1.

The vowels of the IPA may be considered more challenging than the consonants as you must learn a new sound/symbol system for the majority of them. For instance, the "a, e, i, u" do not represent the traditional vowel sounds. In addition, the IPA uses /ɪ/ /ʊ/ /æ/ /ɛ/ /ɝ/ /ɚ/ /ʌ/ /ə/ /ɔ/. You will be relieved to learn that the "o" is represented by the familiar /o/ in the IPA, although some phoneticians use the /oʊ/ to represent "o." As you can see, the vowels of the IPA can be confusing. Similarly, the diphthongs present another sound difference. The diphthongs are written as a combination of two vowel sounds fused together, for example, the /aɪ/ in the word "island." Other diphthongs include /aʊ/ as in "**out**," /ɔɪ/ as in "**coy**," and /ju/ as in "**cute**." IPA symbols for

English vowels and dipthongs are shown in Table 1–2.

You are learning a new, exciting language—it will take time and study, but your efforts will be rewarded as you master transcription with the IPA!

Why Is It Important to Study Phonetics?

Phonetics, the study of speech sounds, is an extremely useful (and mandatory!) tool for the speech-language pathologist. The *International Phonetic Alphabet* (IPA) is used to transcribe, or record using the IPA, the speech of a client. Transcribing the speech errors of a child or adult is an integral part of the assessment process.

Recording of the client's speech using the IPA enables another professional to identify how speech sounds have been produced.

How Speech Sounds Can Be Studied

One of the ways in which speech sounds can be studied is as isolated, separate, and independent entities. Another way speech sounds can be studied is by comparing one sound with another sound. In this Workbook, we will discuss the system of speech sounds classified as Standard American English (SAE), the major dialect of English spoken in the United States of America. Refer to Chapter 16 for a definition of SAE.

A detailed study of speech sounds involves three reference points: (a) the organs that produce speech and their function in producing speech sounds (*physiological phonetics*), (b) the physical properties of the individual speech sounds (*acoustic phonetics*), and (c) the process by which the individual speech sounds are perceived and identified (*percep-

Table 1–1. English Consonants and Their IPA Symbols

Primary Allographic or Orthographic Symbol	IPA Symbol	Key Words
p	/p/	pal, apart, tap
b	/b/	barn, cabin, rub
t	/t/	tea, water, aunt
d	/d/	dish, lady, sand
k	/k/	card, bacon, hook
g	/g/	game, sugar, bag
f	/f/	feed, afford, elf
v	/v/	van, envy, have
th	/θ/	thin, something, cloth
th	/ð/	this, weather, bathe
s	/s/	sat, lesson, horse
z	/z/	zone, puzzle, hose
sh	/ʃ/	ship, fashion, mash
zh	/ʒ/	treasure, beige
h	/h/	hit, behave
wh	/hw/	which, nowhere
ch	/tʃ/	chip, scratching, pitch
j	/dʒ/	jam, magic, page
w	/w/	wet, sandwich
y	/j/	yard, beyond
l	/l/	leaf, mellow, hill
r	/r/	rake, carrot, or
m	/m/	men, camel, time
n	/n/	net, dinner, pine
ng	/ŋ/	ringer, ring

tual phonetics). Physiological phonetics will be the focus of this Workbook as discussed in Chapter 2.

Regardless of the setting in which a speech-language pathologist is employed, a thorough knowledge of phonetics is essential. For instance, it is not uncommon for a speech-language pathologist employed in a school setting to use phonetics daily. Considering the importance of phonetics as a *functional* tool, it has always puzzled the authors that only one semester of undergraduate phonetics is required for majors in speech-language pathology in the United States. In the United Kingdom, four courses in phonetics are required!

Table 1–2. English Vowels and Their IPA Symbols

Primary Allographic or Orthographic Symbol	IPA Symbol	Key Words
ee	/i/	eat, keep, free
-i-	/ɪ/	in, mitt, city
-e-	/ɛ/	ebb, net
-a-	/æ/	at, bat, ham
a-e	/e/	age, face, say
-ur-	/ɝ/ (stressed)	earn, herd, fur
	/ɚ/ (unstressed)	herder, percent
-u-	/ʌ/ (stressed)	up, cup, done
	/ə/ (unstressed)	alive, relative, sofa
-oo-	/u/	boot, stew, soup
-oo-	/ʊ/	hood, could, cook
-aw-	/ɔ/	all, yawn, paw
-o-	/ɑ/	on, bomb
oa	/o/	oak, pole, toe
ou	/aʊ/	ouch, gown, how
i-e	/aɪ/	ice, shine, rye
oi	/ɔɪ/	oyster, loin, toy
u	/ju/	use, cue, mew

CHAPTER

2

Description of the IPA

Studying this chapter will familiarize you with the symbols of the IPA and how to write them correctly. The only way to become comfortable with writing the unfamiliar symbols is to practice, practice, practice! In addition, exercises are provided for you to learn the distinction between the spelling of a word (orthography) and how the word *sounds*.

An important part of learning phonetics is the ability to identify the position of a phoneme in a word. Terms used to describe the position of a sound in a word vary. Words can be divided into syllables, with "V" indicating a vowel and "C" indicating a consonant. For example, the word "sold" is a one-syllable word with the CVCC classification. An example of a two-syllable word is "soda," which would be identified as CVCV.

Consonants have been viewed as appearing in one of three positions in a word: at the beginning of a word (*initial position*) or the first sound heard, the middle of a word *(medial position),* and at the end of a word *(final position)* or the last sound heard. Another classification system identifies a consonant that occurs *before* a vowel as a *prevocalic* consonant, one that occurs *between* two vowels as an *intervocalic* consonant,

and a consonant that occurs *following* a vowel as a *postvocalic* consonant. Locate the /l/ phoneme in the words "look," "alone" and "cool":

Initial Position or Prevocalic: look

Medial Position or Intervocalic: alone

Final Position or Postvocalic: cool

The prevocalic and postvocalic classification system is useful in classifying position of consonant clusters. A *cluster*, also known as a *blend*, is two or more consonants within the same syllable. These can occur in prevocalic or postvocalic positions. Table 3–3 in the following chapter provides examples of consonant clusters.

Recently, consonant locations have been described in terms of their functions rather than their specific location in a word. Consonants can be viewed as performing only two functions, *releasing* vowels or *arresting* vowels. In the word "soap" the consonant /s/ releases the vowel /o/ while the consonant /p/ stops or arrests the vowel.

Bernthal and Bankson (1998) specify the *initial, medial, final* word position as the system used most often for sound-position descriptors. In this Workbook, an initial, medial and final identification exercise has been provided for each IPA phoneme. The words in these exercises were selected to increase your listening ability and to reinforce the difference between the way a word is spelled and how it is pronounced. You will find that the specific phoneme may not always occur in the word examples. These exercises can be heard on the audio CDs. Students who are learning English as a second language should find these exercises particularly useful.

Utilizing the Phoneme Study Cards will also help you to learn the IPA sound/symbol association, which is the foundation for learning phonetics. See below for directions for Phoneme Study Card use.

Directions for Study Card Use

The Phoneme Study Cards that accompany this book are an essential tool in the mastery of the sound/symbol association of the International Phonetic Alphabet.

Each card is numbered. Corresponding numbers are cited in the Transcription Exercises to help you identify the phoneme. You can also listen to the Study Cards on CD 2, Tracks 42–88.

Here are some suggestions for using these cards:

1 Learn the *sound* of the IPA phoneme shown on the front of the card.

2 Memorize the phonetic description for each phoneme.

3 Become familiar with the word-position examples.

4 Create phonetically transcribed words by using the cards.

5 Challenge yourself to reduce the amount of time it takes to identify the sound of each phoneme.

6 Drill, drill, drill!

The "Familiar" IPA Consonants

It is *essential* that you write the symbols of the IPA correctly. If you do not write the symbols correctly, another professional will not be able to read your transcription (Figure 2–1). This is critical because all your referrals (a) to yourself during reassessment and treatment, (b) to your professional colleagues, and (c) to your supervisors must exactly reflect the same information.

"P/p" is written as	*p*
"B/b" is written as	*b*
"K/k" is written as	*k*
"G/g" is written as	*g*
"T/t" is written as	*t*
"D/d" is written as	*d*
"S/s" is written as	*s*
"Z/z" is written as	*z*
"W/w" is written as	*w*
"F/f" is written as	*f*
"V/v" is written as	*v*
"R/r" is written as	*r*
"J/j" is written as	*j*
"H/h" is written as	*h*
"L/l" is written as	*l*
"M/m" is written as	*m*
"N/n" is written as	*n*

Figure 2–1. Familiar IPA consonants.

The "Unfamiliar" IPA Consonants

These consonants may seem very strange, but you will become much more at ease with them as you continue your study of phonetics (see Figure 2–2).

The Vowels of the IPA

The vowels of the IPA may seem confusing at first, but practice will help (see Figure 2–3)! Remember: Do not be confused by spelling, but keep in mind the *sound* of the vowel.

How Do I Write the /æ/?

1 Write the schwa, starting at the top of the letter (Figure 2–4): /ə/ ə

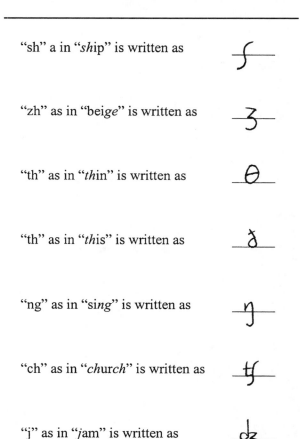

"sh" a in "*sh*ip" is written as

"zh" as in "bei*g*e" is written as

"th" as in "*th*in" is written as

"th" as in "*th*is" is written as

"ng" as in "si*ng*" is written as

"ch" as in "*ch*ur*ch*" is written as

"j" as in "*j*am" is written as

Figure 2–2. Unfamiliar IPA consonants.

The short "i" as in "z*i*p" is written as ɪ

The long "e" as in "k*ee*p" is written as i

The short "e" as in "b*e*t" is written as ɛ

The short "a" as in "c*a*t" is written as æ

The long "a" as in "*a*pe" is written as e

The "ah" sound as in "s*o*d" is written as ɑ

The "uh" sound as in "c*u*p" is written as ʌ

The schwa as in "*a*bout" is written as ə

The "oo" as in "s*ou*p" is written as u

The "oo" as in "c*oo*k" is written as ʊ

The "o" as in "b*oa*t" is written as o

The "aw" as in "p*aw*" is written as ɔ

The "er" as in "h*er*d" is written as ɝ

The "er" as in "herd*er*" is written as ɚ

Figure 2–3. Vowels of the IPA

1. ə   ə   2. æ   æ

Figure 2–4. Writing the ash.

2 Without lifting your pencil from the paper, continue writing the letter "e":

The Diphthongs of the IPA

These will probably seem the strangest of all the IPA symbols, but they are necessary to correctly transcribe words. In addition, the diphthongs are written with a slur (‿) underneath them (Figure 2–5).

"ie" as in "p*ie*" is written as

"ou" as in "c*ow*" is written as

"oy" as in "b*oy*" is written as

"u" as in "v*iew*" is written as

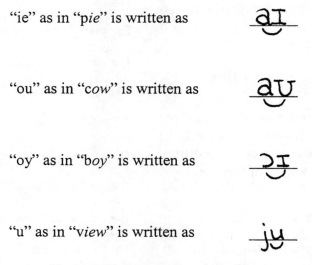

Figure 2–5. Diphthongs of the IPA.

Transcription Exercise 2–1.   **Track: (CD 1, Track 2)**

It is important that you develop the skill to determine the number of *sounds* contained in a word. Count how many sounds each word contains. Listen to CD 1, Track 2 to hear these words pronounced. The Examples section should be helpful to you.

Examples

noisy has 4 sounds: n ɔɪ z i

cough has 3 sounds: k ɑ f

together has 6 sounds: t u g ɛ ð ɚ

ship has 3 sounds: ʃ ɪ p

knife has 3 sounds: n aɪ f

giraffe has 4 sounds: dʒ ɝ æ f

baked has 4 sounds: b e k t

phantom has 6 sounds: f æ n t ə m

might has 3 sounds: m aɪ t

anniversary has 9 sounds: æ n ɪ v ɝ s ə r i

write has 3 sounds: r aɪ t

long has 3 sounds: l ɑ ŋ

Note: "ng" is transcribed: ŋ

whole has 3 sounds: h o l

"x" has 3 sounds: ɛ ks

measure has 4 sounds: m ɛ ʒ ɚ

gnat has 3 sounds: n æ t

Sounds		Transcription
_____	1. gnaw	[_____]
_____	2. shape	[_____]
_____	3. cousin	[_____]
_____	4. leisure	[_____]
_____	5. tongue	[_____]
_____	6. who	[_____]
_____	7. rather	[_____]
_____	8. tough	[_____]
_____	9. kneel	[_____]
_____	10. ax	[_____]
_____	11. cinnamon	[_____]
_____	12. wrap	[_____]
_____	13. raked	[_____]
_____	14. sight	[_____]
_____	15. phoneme	[_____]

Transcription Exercise 2–2.   **Track: (CD 1, Track 3)**

Phoneme Fill-In Exercise

Directions: Using the IPA, write the first *sound* in each of the following words:

1. push   _____

2. real   _____

3. act   _____

4. key   _____

5. top   _____

6. in   _____

7. see   _____

8. every   _____

9. very   _____

10. urge   _____

11. easy   _____

12. dog   _____

13. able   _____

Write the letters and see what they spell:

Transcription Exercise 2–3.   **Track: (CD 1, Track 4)**

Phoneme Identification Exercise

This introductory exercise in phoneme identification is designed to fine-tune your listening abilities. Listen to each word and write the phoneme common to each group of words.

Remember—don't let spelling confuse you!

Consonants   **Phoneme**

1. chorus	Quaker	mannequin	Zachary	physique	/____/
2. tango	kangaroo	Hong Kong	mingle	rectangle	/____/
3. jumbo	effigy	geology	damage	fugitive	/____/
4. phrase	raffle	tough	factory	Ralph	/____/
5. yesterday	papaya	Johann	bayou	savior	/____/
6. misery	hose	adviser	weighs	resume	/____/

Vowels

7. fruit	loop	tube	knew	zoos	/____/
8. eve	cease	free	quiche	beanie	/____/
9. coach	own	robe	beau	throw	/____/
10. birch	hermit	urge	myrtle	fur	/____/
11. bathe	lay	vein	gate	eighty	/____/
12. ah	jaunt	spa	palm	shock	/____/

YOUR FIRST EXERCISE—Transcribe Your Name!

Transcription Rules

Rule 1: Transcribe according to the way your name *sounds,* not how it is *spelled.*

Rule 2: No capital letters for your first, middle, or last name.

Rule 3: Put first, middle, and last names in one set of brackets: [   ].

Rule 4: No double phonetic symbols—remember, it is how your name sounds, not how many letters are used.

Helpful Hints

- Be sure to use the Study Cards to help you make the sound-symbol connection.
- Your phonetics instructor can review your transcription and make helpful suggestions.

JUST FOR FUN

Transcribe the names of family members, pets, favorite actors, and sports figures.

3

Articulatory Aspects of Phonetics

A review of basic anatomy and physiology is helpful for the beginning phonetics student as a basic understanding of speech production provides a necessary background for production of each phoneme. Keep in mind that this chapter provides a *brief* review.

The study of phonetics that describes the physiological properties of speech is called *physiological phonetics.* Various speech organs, such as the tongue, lips, teeth, and soft palate, can be positioned to create a wide variety of speech sounds simply by making small adjustments in the movements and locations of the speech organs within the oral cavity. These movements are performed automatically in the accomplished speaker and may become extremely complex in form.

The primary purpose of the structures used for speech is survival. For example, the lungs are the source of respiration, but they also provide a breathstream for speech. The tongue helps move the bolus of food to the posterior portion of the mouth so that the food can be swallowed, but it also produces speech sounds. The body parts used for speech production can be considered a speech-producing mechanism. Refer to Figure 3–1 and Figure 3–2 for an illustration of these body parts.

Larynx: The larynx is located in the throat, just above the trachea. It extends to the top of the esophagus, which is below the root of the tongue. Housed in the larynx are the *vocal folds.* The space between the vocal folds is the *glottis.* When the vocal folds **adduct,** or *close,* they vibrate to provide voicing for speech. When the folds **abduct,** or *open,* they do not vibrate and voicing is not produced. Refer to Figure 3–3 for an illustration of the vocal folds.

Pharynx: A tubular, funnel-shaped structure located posterior to the root of the tongue and extending downward to the esophagus. The pharynx is divided into three parts: the nasopharynx, oropharynx, and the laryngopharynx (see Figure 3–2).

Nasopharynx: Section of the pharynx that lies directly posterior to the nasal cavity. Extends anteriorly from the nostrils to the posterior wall of the pharynx.

Oropharynx: Section of the pharynx that is directly posterior to the oral cavity

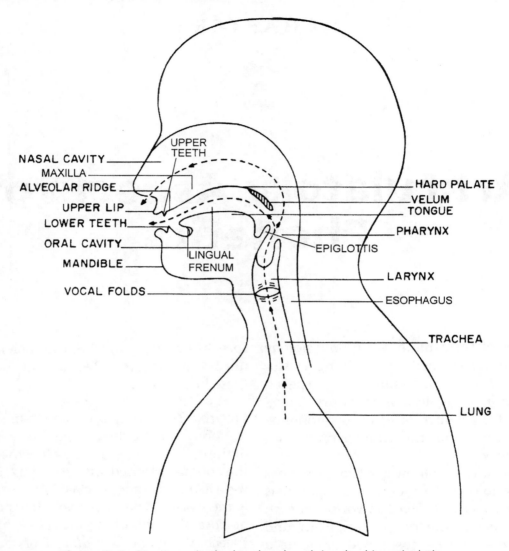

Figure 3–1. Structures in the head and neck involved in articulation.

and extends from the level of the velum above to the level or the root of the tongue below. Can be easily viewed when the mouth is wide open and the tongue is pulled forward.

Laryngopharynx: The lower part of the pharynx which lies directly behind the laryngeal structures.

The pharynx contains two valves: the velopharyngeal valve and the epiglottal valve.

Velopharyngeal valve: Located at the juncture of the oropharynx and the

nasopharynx. When this valve activates, it closes the nasopharynx and obstructs the laryngeal airstream from entering the nasopharynx and the nasal cavity.

Epiglottal valve: Located just below the root of the tongue at the juncture of the oropharynx and the laryngopharynx. The epiglottis acts like a cover for the opening of the larynx during the passage of food from the oral cavity into the esophagus.

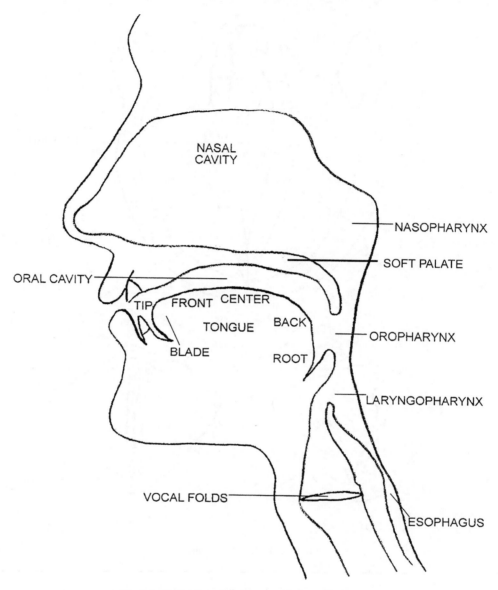

Figure 3–2. Resonating cavities and tongue.

Oral cavity: The *oropharynx* opens anteriorly into the *oral cavity*. The oral cavity is bounded anteriorly by the lips and laterally by the cheeks. The tongue rests on the floor of the oral cavity. The hard palate and the velum form the roof of the oral cavity.

Lips: The upper and lower lips are made of muscles that have a great degree of mobility, facilitating the formation of various lip shapes for the production of vowels such as /ɑ,o,ʊ,æ/ and consonants, such as /p,b,m,w,hw,f,v/.

Teeth: The upper and lower teeth lie posterior to the lips. The upper and lower incisors, in particular, play an important role in the production of some consonants. The consonants involving both upper and lower incisors are /θ,ð/ and the consonants involving only the lower incisors are /f,v/.

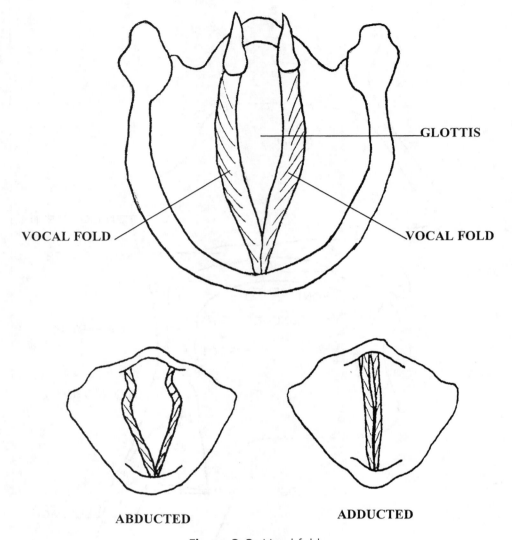

Figure 3–3. Vocal folds.

Alveolar ridge: This structure is located behind the upper and lower teeth and is also known as the *gum ridge*. It serves as the point of contact or approximation for the tongue tip or front of the tongue in the production of numerous speech sounds such as the /t,d,l,s,z/.

Hard palate: The anterior two thirds of the roof of the mouth is arched and comprises the bony *hard palate*. The hard palate serves as the point of contact, or the point of approximation, for the front of the tongue in the production of speech sounds such as /ʃ,ʒ,j/.

Velum: The posterior one third of the palate. It is soft and muscular. It is also known as the soft palate. The velum serves as the point of contact for the back of the tongue in the production of speech sounds such as /k,g,ŋ/. The velum, aided somewhat by the posterior pharyngeal wall musculature, forms a valve known as the *velopharyngeal valve.*

This valve opens and closes the port between the nasopharynx and the oropharynx. When the valve is open, the speech sounds produced have a nasal resonance caused by the passage of a portion of the laryngeal airstream through the nasal cavity, as in the production of English consonants /m,n,ŋ/. However, the valve is usually closed during the production of speech sounds that do not require nasal resonance, as in the production of English vowels and non-nasal consonants.

Tongue: Derived from the Latin word *"lingua,"* the tongue is an exclusively muscular organ that rests on the floor of the oral cavity. It is an extremely mobile organ capable of making innumerable changes in positioning and muscle tension guided by the action of the intrinsic (originating inside the tongue) and extrinsic (originating outside the tongue muscles). All vowels are influenced by tongue position. The only consonants that do not have direct tongue involvement are: /m,p,b,f,v/.

Lingual frenum: Small, white cord of tissue. This tissue extends from the floor of the oral cavity to the midline of the under surface of the tongue blade. A frenum that is too short may restrict production of sounds which require tongue elevation.

Maxilla: The upper jaw which forms the majority of the palate.

Mandible: The lower jaw. Helps to move the lower teeth close to or away from the upper teeth. Its movement helps to reduce or enlarge the size of the oral cavity. The maximum downward movement of the mandible is seen during the production of the English vowel /æ/.

Lungs: The lungs are the organ of respiration and provide a breathstream for speech. Speech is produced when the breathstream is exhaled, or expelled, from the lungs.

Trachea: Rings comprised of cartilage and membranes leading from the larynx into the lungs; often referred to as the "windpipe."

Speech Processes

Speech is the end product of the four processes of **Phonation**, **Articulation**, **Respiration**, and **Resonance** (PARR).

Phonation is accomplished with the rhythmic and rapid opening and closing of the vocal folds, which open or close the glottis.

Articulation is how the breathstream is modified to form speech sounds.

Respiration provides the flow of air for speech, which is exhalation.

Resonation is the process of vibrating air in a resonating cavity. The resonating cavities were discussed earlier in this chapter.

Articulatory Aspects of Consonants

The production of consonants can be described by the *place* of articulation (*where* the phoneme is produced), the *manner* of articulation (*how* the breathstream is modified as it passes through the oral cavity), and *voicing* (if the vocal folds adduct for a voiced phoneme or abduct for an unvoiced phoneme). The majority of the consonants of the IPA are *cognates*, which means the phonemes are made in the same place and in the same manner, with the only difference being in voicing.

Each phoneme in the IPA is identified by place, manner, voicing, and distinctive features. Distinctive features will be discussed later in this chapter. As you review each phoneme page, you will find the phoneme described by manner, place, voicing, and distinctive features.

Place of Articulation

Figure 3–4 illustrates the oral cavity shapes for the places of articulation.

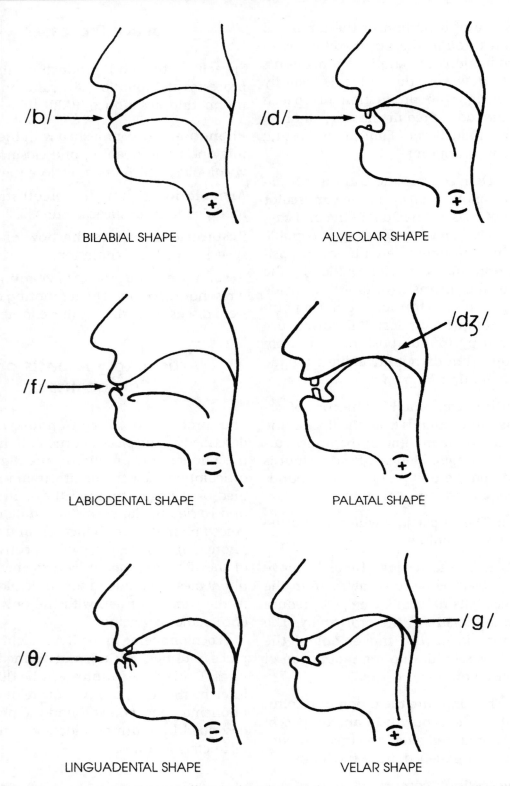

BILABIAL SHAPE

ALVEOLAR SHAPE

LABIODENTAL SHAPE

PALATAL SHAPE

LINGUADENTAL SHAPE

VELAR SHAPE

Figure 3–4. Diagram showing the six different alterations in the oral cavity shape controlled by lip and tongue contacts at the six different places along the horizontal line of the oral cavity. Plus sign (+) indicates presence of voicing; minus (–) sign indicates absence of voicing.

Bilabial: Sounds produced at the lips are known as *labial* sounds. The English phonemes /p/, /b/, /m/, /w/, and /hw/ are classified as bilabials because both (or *bi-*) lips are used to produce them. The upper and lower lips serve as *articulators*, which are movable speech organs involved in the shaping of speech sounds. Only the lower lip is involved in production of /f/ and /v/.

Labiodental: The /f/ and /v/ phonemes are classified as *labio-* (meaning lip) *-dental* (meaning teeth) as the lip and teeth produce those phonemes.

Linguadental: *Lingua-* (meaning tongue) *-dental* (teeth) sounds are produced when the tip of the tongue is between the upper and lower teeth. These phonemes /θ/ and /ð/ are also referred to as interdentals, reflecting the tongue tip position between the upper and lower teeth.

Alveolar: The *alveolar* ridge (see Figure 3–1) is a very important point of tongue contact in many world languages, including English. Numerous sounds are produced when the tongue tip touches the alveolar ridge. The /t/, /d/, /n/, /s/, /z/, /l/, and /r/ are classified as lingua-alveolar phonemes.

Palatal: The consonants /ʃ/, /ʒ/, /tʃ/, /dʒ/, and /j/ are produced by the body of the tongue contacting, or approximating, the posterior portion of the hard palate.

Velar: The consonants /k/, /g/, and /ŋ/ are classified as lingua-velar sounds when the back portion of the tongue contacts the velum, or soft palate.

Glottal: The /h/ phoneme is classified as a glottal because it is produced when the vocal folds partially adduct to create friction or turbulence. The tongue does not assume any specific position in the oral cavity, and may be in position to produce the sound that follows the /h/.

Table 3–1 summarizes place of articulation.

Manner of Articulation

Manner of articulation describes *how* speech sounds are produced. The articulators are positioned and must react in a specific way to produce the phoneme. Ways in which consonants are produced are described by the terms in Figure 3–5. Looking at this figure, you will note that a consonant can belong to more than one category.

Table 3–1. Places of Articulation

CONSONANT	PLACE OF ARTICULATION	ARTICULATORS
/ p, b, m, w /	Bilabial	Lips
/ f, v /	Labiodental	Lower lip and upper teeth
/ θ, ð /	Linguadental	Tip of tongue and teeth
/ t, d, n, s, z, l, r /	Alveolar	Tip of tongue and alveolar ridge
/ ʃ, ʒ, tʃ, dʒ, j /	Palatal	Body of tongue and hard palate
/ k, g, ŋ /	Velar	Back of tongue and soft palate
/ h /	Glottal	Adduction/abduction of vocal folds

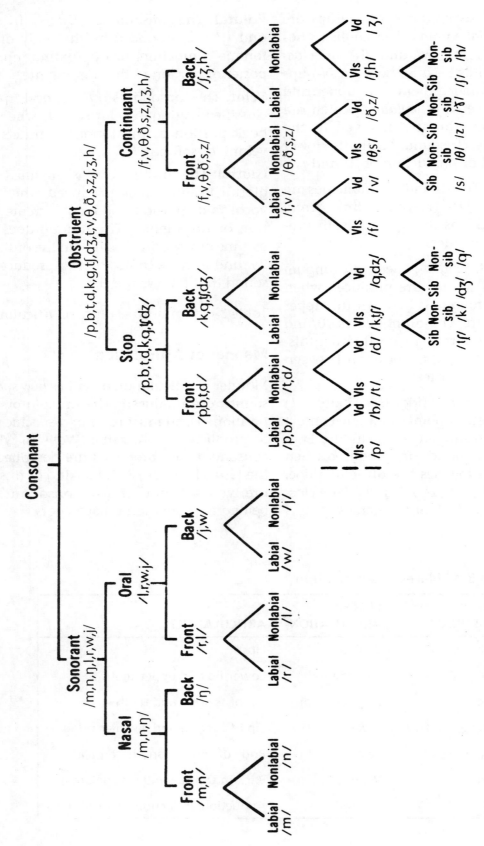

Figure 3–5. Division of consonants, on binary principles, into sonorant/obstruent, nasal/oral, stop/continuant, front/back, labial/nonlabial, voiceless/voiced (Vls/Vd), and sibilant/nonsibilant (Sib/Non-Sib) groups. (Reproduced with permission from *Phonetics: Principles and Practices* [3rd ed.], by S. Singh and K. Singh, 2006, p. 63. Copyright 2006 Plural Publishing, Inc.)

Obstruents: Obstruents are produced with an *obstru*ction in the vocal tract, which can be a complete or incomplete obstruction.

Sonorants: A sonorant is the opposite of an obstruent because the sound passes through a relatively open channel and is not blocked.

Stops: These phonemes are produced with a total blockage of the airstream. In these consonants, the airstream must be released after it is blocked. This class of consonants is also referred to as plosives.

Continuants: Unlike the stops, continuants are produced in a *continu*ing manner, with relatively less obstruction. Contrast production of the /t/ as in "tuh, tuh, tuh," with the continuous flow of air when producing the /s/ as in "s-s-s-s-s."

Fricatives: These phonemes are obstruents because they are produced with a partial blockage of the airstream, resulting in turbulence or *fri*ction.

Affricates: The only affricates in the IPA, /tʃ/ and /dʒ/, begin with production of a stop-consonant and end with production of a fricative.

Orals: This category refers to resonating cavities (see Figure 3–2). The consonants in this group are produced in the resonating cavity of the vocal tract excluding the nasal cavity and nasopharynx.

Nasals: The /m/, /n/, and /ŋ/ are the only consonants requiring nasal resonance. The resonating cavity is the entire vocal tract, including the nasal cavity and the nasopharynx. Nasal resonance is accomplished by the lowering of the velum to permit airflow into the nasal cavity.

Liquids and glides: The consonants /r/, /l/, /w/, and /j/ are considered liquids and glides because of their extreme flexibility in assuming the role of either a consonant or a vowel. The /l/ is also called a lateral because it is the only phoneme with airflow around the *sides* of the tongue.

Voiced and voiceless: This category focuses on the vibration of the vocal folds. For a voiced phoneme, the vocal folds are *add*ucted and vibrate. For voiceless sounds, the vocal folds are *ab*ducted and no voicing is produced.

Articulatory Aspects of Vowels

Vowel classification differs greatly from the system used to classify consonants. Vowels are classified by tongue position (refer to Figure 9–1). All vowels require voicing produced by the vibrating vocal folds. Refer to Chapter 9 for more information about vowels.

Distinctive Features

Distinctive features are those attributes of a phoneme that are required to differentiate one phoneme from another in a language. For example, the phonemes /k/ and /g/ in English are differentiated by the feature of voicing, which in turn is an attribute in differentiating phonemes in the English language. Figure 3–6 displays distinctive feature contrast for English consonants. The features are:

Voicing/voiceless: The vocal folds *add*uct for a voiced phoneme and *ab*duct for a voiceless phoneme.

Front/back: The consonant is produced in the front of the vocal tract (lips, alveolar ridge) or in the back of the vocal tract (hard or soft palate).

Labial/nonlabial: One or both lips are used in producing the consonant or the lips are not used to form the sound.

Sonorant/nonsonorant: The relatively open vocal tract is used to produce a sonorant consonant; nonsonorant refers to an obstructed vocal tract.

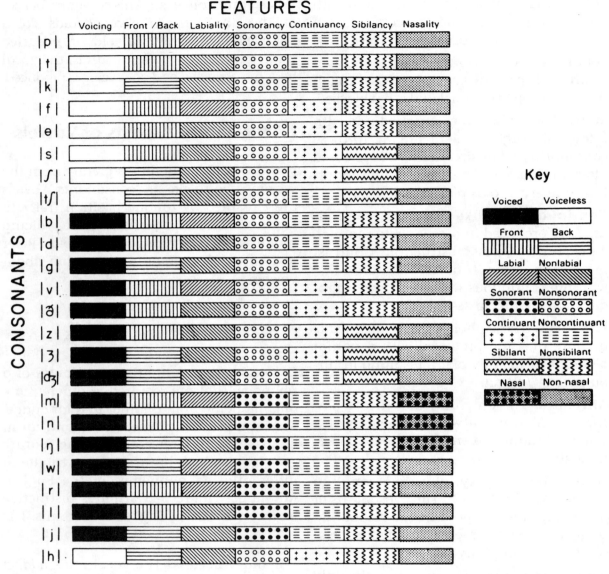

Figure 3–6. A visual description of distinctive feature contrast among English consonants. (Reprinted with permission from *Phonetics: Principles and Practices* [3rd ed.], by S. Singh and K. Singh, 2006, p. 168. Copyright 2006 Plural Publishing, Inc.)

Continuant/noncontinuant: Continuant phonemes are made without a constriction so that the airflow is not blocked. A noncontinuant sound is constricted.

Sibilant/nonsibilant: Consonants with this distinctive feature have a "hissing" sound such as the /s/ or /ʃ/.

Nasal/non-nasal: Nasal consonants require nasal resonance through lowering of the velopharyngeal port to allow the airflow into the nasal cavity.

Ages of Consonant Development

Table 3–2 presents data summarized from several studies indicating ages of consonant development. You will note variation in age of acquisition of the various consonants.

Table 3–2. Ages of Consonant Development (in years)

Consonant	Wellman et al. (1931)	Poole (1934)	Templin (1957)	Praether et al. (1975)	Arlt & Goodban (1976)
m	3	3½	3	2	3
n	3	4½	3	2	3
h	3	3½	3	2	3
p	4	3½	3	2	3
f	3	5½	3	2–4	3
w	3	3½	3	2–8	3
b	3	3½		2–8	3
ŋ		4½	3	2–8	3
j	4	4½	3½	2–4	
k	4	4½	4	2–4	3
g	4	4½	4	2–4	3
l	4	6½	6	3–4	4
d	5	4½	4	2–4	3
t	5	4½	6	2–8	3
s	5	7½	4½	3	4
r	5	7½	4	3	5
tʃ	5	4½		3–8	4
v	5	6½	6	4	3½
z	5	7½	7	4	4
ʒ	6	6½	7	4	4
θ		7½	6	4	5
dʒ		7	4	4	
ʃ		6½	4½	3–8	4½
ð		6½	7	4	5

Reprinted with permission from *Assessment and Treatment of Articulation and Phonological Disorders in Children*, by Adriana Pena-Brooks and M. N. Hegde, 2000, p. 71. Copyright 2000 by Pro-Ed, Inc.

Consonant Clusters

A *consonant cluster*, also referred to as a *consonant blend*, is a combination of two or more adjacent consonants in the same syllable. The words "tree" [tri] and "street" [strit] have double and triple consonant clusters, respectively, in the initial position of the word. Clusters can also occur in the medial position (underlined) as in "restrain" [ristren] or in the final position as in "fast" [fæst].

A consonant cluster is simply a way of combining the consonant phonemes in a language. Only certain consonants can be used to form clusters. While initial consonant clusters /st/, /sk/, /sp/, and /sw/ occur in English, clusters such as /sb/, /sd/, /sg/, /sr/, and /sv/ are not found in the initial position of a word in English. Table 3–3 provides numerous examples of clusters in Standard American English in the initial (syllable-initiating) and final (syllable-terminating) positions.

Table 3–3. Examples of Consonant Clusters in American English

Consonant Cluster	Sample Allographic Representations	Consonant Cluster	Sample Allographic Representations
Syllable-Initiating		**Syllable-Terminating**	
kw-	quick, queen, quack, quantity	-mp	ramp, lamp, stomp
tw-	tweezers, twist, twang, twenty	-nt	ant, pleasant, count, plant
sw-	swim, sweat, swap, sweeten	-nd	hand, bend, fond, blind
pl-	play, plan, plastic, place	-ns	prince, cleanse
kl-	Clown, clock, clap, clean	-rd	hard, weird, guard, chard
fl-	flag, flick, flounder, flack	-nz	lens, plans, buns
bl-	black, blast, blink, Blake	-ks	parks, lacks, plaques
gl-	glasses, gloat, glimpse, glad	-st	past, best, post, nest
sl-	slide, slap, slender, sleep	-kt	act, fact, deduct, induct
pr-	prize, present, practical, prepare	-ld	held, mold, peeled
br-	brown, brag, brain, bring	-rt	art, fort, mart, sort
tr-	truck, tree, train, trap	-ts	bets, mats, ports
dr-	drive, drink, drastic, dramatic	-rn	barn, burn, fern, churn
fr-	front, frog, frost, French	-rm	arm, farm, alarm, charm
r-	through, threat, thrive	-lb	bulb
kr-	crown, crop, create, creep	-lp	pulp, help, gulp
gr-	green, gray, grass, gripe	-lt	halt, malt, fault
st-	stop, steel, steak, stork	-lf	half, calf
sp-	spot, sport, speak, Spanish	-lk	bulk, stalk, walk
sk-	school, scar, score, Scott	-rst	burst, first
sn-	snake, snow, sniff, snack	-zd	buzzed, blazed
sm-	small, smile, smack, smudge	-rk	park, mark, fork
nj-	news, newsworthy, newcomer	-mz	arms, aims, stems
fj-	few, fugitive, fumes, future	-lz	balls, malls, steals
kj-	cute, coupon, accused	-gz	bugs, pegs
mj-	music, amused, musician	-pt	opt, stopped, dropped
f-	shrink, shriek, shrine	-ft	left, stuffed, lift
str-	stray, street, strong, strange	-rf	scarf
skw-	squander, squat, squint	-rv	starve, carve, swerve
spl-	splash, splendor, splint	-mpt	stomped, stamped
spr-	spray, sprint, sprinkle	-mps	lamps, cramps, blimps
skr-	scram, scream, screech	-nts	ants, pants, prints
		-ngz	strings
		-ndz	hands, grounds

Reprinted with permission from *Assessment and Treatment of Articulation and Phonological Disorders in Children*, by Adriana Pena-Brooks and M. N. Hegde, 2000, p. 138 Copyright 2000 by Pro-Ed, Inc.

4

Stop-Consonants

Stop-consonants, also known as plosives, require a stopping of the breathstream by a closure within the oral cavity. Production of a stop-consonant is a *manner* of articulation. Manner of articulation was discussed in Chapter 3. There are two phases involved in production of a stop-consonant: the air must be stopped and then it must be released. Stopping of the air is mandatory, as air must be held in the oral cavity. The plosive phase of the stop releases the impounded air. Stopping of the airstream can occur by lip closure, as in producing /b/, tongue elevation, as in production of /t/, or by adduction of the vocal folds for a glottal stop.

Release of the air, also known as aspiration, can occur in two ways. The air can be released as a "puff" of air, similar to that of an ex*plosion*, when released into a vowel as in the word "pay" [pʰe] or released without the explosion of air as in the phrase "at work." The symbol [ʰ] identifies aspiration of the impounded air and the [˺] denotes unreleased air.

The glottal stop is not considered a phoneme but is a dialectal or allophonic variation of /t/ and /k/. It is written as ʔ. The glottal stop is produced by the vocal folds when they *ad*duct to hold air in the glottis and *ab*duct to release the air. Transcription Exercise 4–7 will give you examples of a glottal stop and an opportunity for hearing the difference between the /t/ and the glottal stop.

/p/

Transcription Exercise 4–1   **Track: (CD 1, Track 5)**

		I	M	F
1.	phone			
2.	split			
3.	hiccough			
4.	gopher			
5.	shopping			
6.	president			
7.	peppermint			
8.	pneumatic			
9.	append			
10.	pamphlet			

Transcription Exercise 4–2
Consonant: /p/

 Track: (CD 1, Track 6)
Refer to Study Card: 3

Phonetic Symbol	Target Word	Transcription
/p/	1. pine	
	2. deep	
	3. oppose	
	4. cape	
	5. paper	
	6. sip	
	7. place	
	8. help	
	9. pack	

/p/

Distinctive Features	Tongue Position
Bilabial stop consonant Voiceless, front, labial, nonsonorant, noncontinuant, nonsibilant, non-nasal 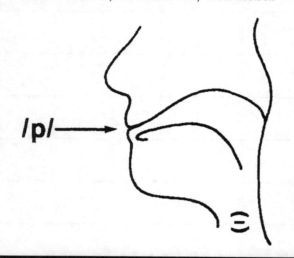	Not relevant for production of this phoneme. May be in position for following consonant or vowel. Lips are closed. Breath is held and compressed in oral cavity. Breathstream may or may not be released with aspiration; dependent upon surrounding consonants and syllable position.

Voicing/Velopharyngeal Port	Spelling Variations
Voiceless—vocal folds *ab*duct. VP port is closed.	Appears as /p/ in words Appears in clusters with /l/r/s/spl/spr/ pp in medial position (*apply/oppose*) is transcribed with a single /p/ This phoneme may be intruded in the following words if an unvoiced phoneme follows a nasal: warmth [wormpθ] comfort [kʌmpfɚt] dreamt [drɛmpt]

Word Position	Clinical Information
Initial, medial, and final positions in SAE	Cognate of /b/

/b/

Transcription Exercise 4–3   Track: (CD 1, Track 7)

		I	M	F
1.	humble			
2.	ribbon			
3.	belabor			
4.	public			
5.	Burbank			
6.	thumb			
7.	probe			
8.	halibut			
9.	broke			
10.	tombstone			

Transcription Exercise 4–4
Consonant: /b/

 Track: (CD 1, Track 8)
Refer to Study Card: 4

Phonetic Symbol	Target Word	Transcription
/b/	1. bad	
	2. tub	
	3. baby	
	4. bright	
	5. rabbit	
	6. nobody	
	7. bomb	
	8. cob	
	9. curb	

/b/

Distinctive Features	Tongue Position
Bilabial stop consonant Voiced, front, labial, nonsonorant, noncontinuant, nonsibilant, non-nasal /b/ →	Irrelevant; tongue may be in position for following consonant or vowel. Lips are closed. Breath is held and compressed in oral cavity. Breathstream may or may not be released with aspiration; dependent upon surrounding consonants and syllable position.

Voicing/Velopharyngeal Port	Spelling Variations
Voiced—Vocal folds *adduct*. VP port is closed.	bb in medial position (ho*bb*y, ru*bb*er) is transcribed with a single /b/ pb occurs rarely as /b/ in cu*pb*oard silent /b/ in bom*b*

Word Positions	Clinical Information
Initial, medial, and final positions in SAE	Cognate of /p/

Crossword Puzzle for /p/ and /b/

Answers in Appendix B

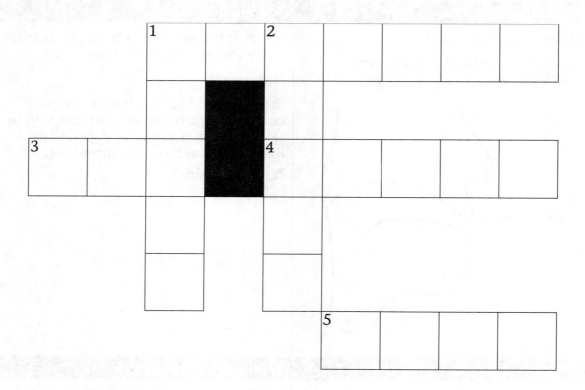

Directions: Transcribe the following words:

Across:
1. pollywog
3. cub
4. pumps
5. bring

Down:
1. pebble
2. leaping

BABYTIME

Word Search # 1   Answers in Appendix B

s	ʃ	r	d	aɪ	p	ɚ	z	b	ɔ	l	t	z	r
d	ʒ	ɝ	k	ʃ	ə	b	p	æ	n	d	ə	ð	ʌ
b	ɑ	t	ə	l	o	r	r	i	æ	k	n	ʊ	d
s	tʃ	i	w	b	l	u	p	m	ɪ	p	z	n	kʍ
h	p	ɛ	t	e	v	i	b	b	e	u	l	m	p
f	ɑ	ʒ	ŋ	b	ɛ	ʌ	ɔ	k	r	ɪ	p	t	s
k	p	t	θ	i	p	z	z	t	dʒ	i	b	v	n
l	ɑ	s	l	z	ð	w	k	m	æ	ʒ	n	æ	p
b	ɛ	f	o	ɪ	ɛ	r	ʃ	ɪ	k	o	u	r	æ
h	b	æ	s	ɪ	n	ɛ	t	r	g	l	ʊ	f	s
n	ɪ	z	ɛ	g	ɔ	ɪ	ʌ	i	d	r	s	n	ɪ
s	b	e	b	ɪ	b	n	z	b	ʌ	n	i	g	f
p	ɪ	ŋ	k	w	dʒ	ð	b	e	ʌ	ɛ	ɪ	ʒ	aɪ
j	f	e	ɪ	w	ə	p	r	w	ɝ	g	v	z	j
l	b	l	æ	ŋ	k	ɛ	t	p	t	d	i	ɔ	ɚ
r	g	h	p	ks	f	m	ɚ	b	g	ɑ	r	ə	g

Directions: Find and circle the words listed below which contain the /p/ or /b/ phonemes.

papa	pacifier	bunny	bassinet
panda	bib	diapers	blanket
pink	bottle	blue	nap
baby			

/t/

Transcription Exercise 4–5   Track: (CD 1, Track 9)

		I	M	F
1.	caught			
2.	whistle			
3.	tuition			
4.	thyme			
5.	tentative			
6.	tortilla			
7.	watched			
8.	chalet			
9.	territory			
10.	motion			

Transcription Exercise 4–6
Consonant: /t/

 Track: (CD 1, Track 10)
Refer to Study Card: 5

Phonetic Symbol	Target Word	Transcription
/t/	1. tube	
	2. cut	
	3. into	
	4. until	
	5. twin	
	6. coat	
	7. rotate	
	8. time	
	9. nest	

/t/

Distinctive Features	Tongue Position
Lingua-alveolar stop-consonant Voiceless, front, nonlabial, nonsonorant, noncontinuant, nonsibilant, non-nasal 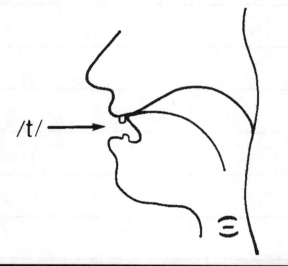 /t/ →	Tip of tongue contacts alveolar ridge with sides against upper molars. Breath is held in oral cavity; may be released with or without aspiration.

Voicing/Velopharyngeal Port	Spelling Variations
Voiceless—vocal folds *ab*duct. VP port is closed.	Usually occurs as /t/. tt transcribed as a single /t/ in medial position as in li*tt*le. -ed following unvoiced consonants as in wish*ed*, cough*ed*, tap*ed* is transcribed with a /t/, except following the /t/ as in ska*ted* or wai*ted*. th as in *Th*omas, *Th*eresa transcribed as /t/. n( )s results in an intruded /t/ sound, not included in spelling, between /n/ and /s/ as in chance [tʃænᵗs] or tense [tɛnᵗs]. t is silent in sof*t*en, cas*t*le, whis*t*le.

Word Position	Clinical Information
Initial, medial, and final positions in SAE	Commonly replaced with the voiced /t/ or glottal stop Cognate of /d/

The Glottal Stop

Transcription Exercise 4–7   **Track: (CD 1, Track 11)**

Remember these things about the glottal stop:

1 It is an allophonic variation of the /t/.

2 Do not confuse the glottal stop with a question mark. It is written as: ?

3 When followed by an "n" in the spelling of the word, a syllabic /n̩/ is used.

Here is a transcription exercise to familiarize you with the glottal stop. Words in the first column are dictated with the /t/. The second column words are dictated with the glottal stop.

Word	/t/ transcription	Glottal stop transcription
1. Doolittle	_____	_____
2. mitten	_____	_____
3. fountain	_____	_____
4. patent	_____	_____
5. Hilton	_____	_____
6. button	_____	_____
7. Latin	_____	_____
8. cotton	_____	_____
9. bitten	_____	_____
10. molten	_____	_____

The Voiced /t/

Transcription Exercise 4–8   Track: (CD 1, Track 12)

Like the glottal stop, the voiced /t/ is an allophonic variation of the /t/. It is an alternative pronunciation. The voiced /t/ can result when voiced phonemes precede and follow the /t/. In the examples that follow, the /t/ in *intervocalic* (between two vowels), and the voiced sounds that surround the /t/ cause it to sound voiced.

Transcribe the following words. Words in the first column are dictated with the /t/. The second column words are dictated with the voiced /t/. Remember that the voiced /t/ sounds like the /d/. Here is a rule for using a voiced /t/: *If a word is spelled with a "t," but you hear a "d," use the "v" (for voicing) /t̬/.*

Word	/t/ transcription	Voiced /t/ transcription
1. better	_____	_____
2. hotter	_____	_____
3. battle	_____	_____
4. matter	_____	_____
5. atom	_____	_____
6. butter	_____	_____
7. cater	_____	_____
8. quota	_____	_____
9. cheated	_____	_____
10. duty	_____	_____

/d/

Transcription Exercise 4–9   Track: (CD 1, Track 13)

		I	M	F
1.	hedge			
2.	handkerchief			
3.	mapped			
4.	deadened			
5.	decade			
6.	pointed			
7.	adding			
8.	medial			
9.	dread			
10.	demand			

Transcription Exercise 4–10
Consonant: /d/

 Track: (CD 1, Track 14)
Refer to Study Card: 6

Phonetic Symbol	Target Word	Transcription
/d/	1. dough	
	2. condition	
	3. used	
	4. dish	
	5. meadow	
	6. sand	
	7. dwell	
	8. wonder	
	9. changed	

/d/

Distinctive Features	Tongue Position
Lingua-alveolar stop-consonant Voiced front, nonlabial, nonsonorant, noncontinuant, nonsibilant, non-nasal /d/ ⟶	Same as for the cognate /t/

Voicing/Velopharyngeal Port	Spelling Variations
Voiced—vocal folds *ad*duct. VP port is closed.	d is primary. dd is transcribed with a /d/ as in *add* or sa*dd*er. -ed has sound of /d/ following vowels as in mow*ed* and pray*ed* and voiced consonants as in sa*ved* or open*ed*. ld occurs with silent /l/ in cou*ld*, shou*ld*.

Word Position	Clinical Information
Initial, medial, and final positions in SAE	Cognate of /t/

Crossword Puzzle for /t/ and /d/

Answer in Appendix B

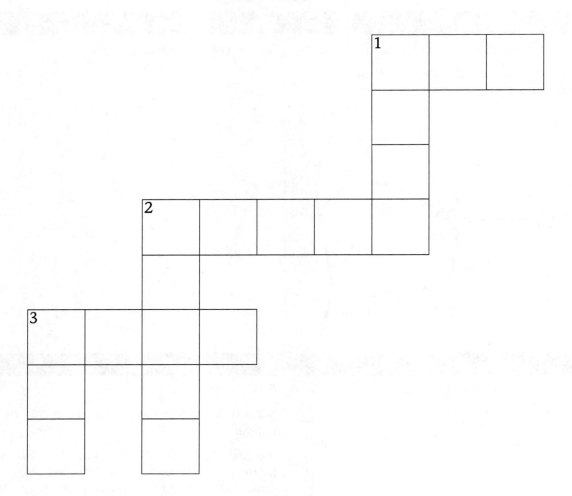

Directions: Transcribe the following words:

Across:

1. deaf
2. disease
3. data

Down:

1. dimes
2. detour
3. dot

/k/

Transcription Exercise 4–11 Track: (CD 1, Track 15)

		I	M	F
1.	centimeter			
2.	pique			
3.	quartet			
4.	text			
5.	bronchitis			
6.	impeccable			
7.	critic			
8.	backache			
9.	knight			
10.	Tocqueville			

Transcription Exercise 4–12
Consonant: /k/

 Track: (CD 1, Track 16)
Refer to Study Card: 1

Phonetic Symbol	Target Word	Transcription
/k/	1. back	
	2. count	
	3. tick	
	4. basket	
	5. cake	
	6. cream	
	7. stocking	
	8. across	
	9. marquee	

/k/

Distinctive Features	Tongue Position
Lingua-velar stop consonant	Back of tongue elevates to touch velum.
Voiceless, back, nonlabial, nonsonorant, noncontinuant, nonsibilant, non-nasal	Air pressure builds up behind tongue/velum seal.
	Lips are apart and neutral.
/k/	Air pressure is released when tongue moves from velum.

Voicing/Velopharyngeal Port	Spelling Variations
Voiceless—vocal folds *ab*duct.	Numerous variations
VP port is closed.	cc as in "o*cc*ur" transcribed with a single /k/.
	ch as in a*ch*e, *ch*orus ck always has /k/ sounds as in du*ck*, ti*ck* que as in techni*que* kh as in *kh*aki
	ng ( ) th results in an intruded /k/, not included in the spelling of the word, as in length. [lɛŋkθ]
	Cluster examples: kl, kr, sk, skw, skr

Word Position	Clinical Information
Initial, medial, and final positions in SAE	/t/ is often substituted for /k/ in young children.
	Cognate of /g/

/g/

Transcription Exercise 4–13   **Track: (CD 1, Track 17)**

		I	M	F
1.	gentle			
2.	garbage			
3.	gnat			
4.	eggnog			
5.	exist			
6.	gouge			
7.	laugh			
8.	Gertrude			
9.	linger			
10.	digit			

Transcription Exercise 4–14
Consonant: /g/

 Track: (CD 1, Track 18)
Refer to Study Card: 2

Phonetic Symbol	Target Word	Transcription
/g/	1. gone	
	2. wiggle	
	3. hungry	
	4. beg	
	5. dog	
	6. green	
	7. vague	
	8. glove	
	9. griddle	

/g/

Distinctive Features	Tongue Position
Lingua-velar stop-consonant	Same as for /k/
Voiced back, nonlabial, nonsonorant, noncontinuant, nonsibilant, non-nasal	

Voicing/Velopharyngeal Port	Spelling Variations
Voiced—vocal folds *ad*duct.	gg transcribed with single /g/ sound.
VP port is closed.	Exception: su*gg*est [sʌgdʒɛst]
	gue as in vo*gue* gu as in *gu*est, *gu*ard gh as in *gh*ost (e)x as in *exist* has the /gz/ sound [ɛgzɪst]

Word Positions	Clinical Information
Initial, medial, and final positions in SAE	Common articulatory substitution: d/g
	Cognate of /k/

Crossword Puzzle for /k/ and /g/

Answers in Appendix B

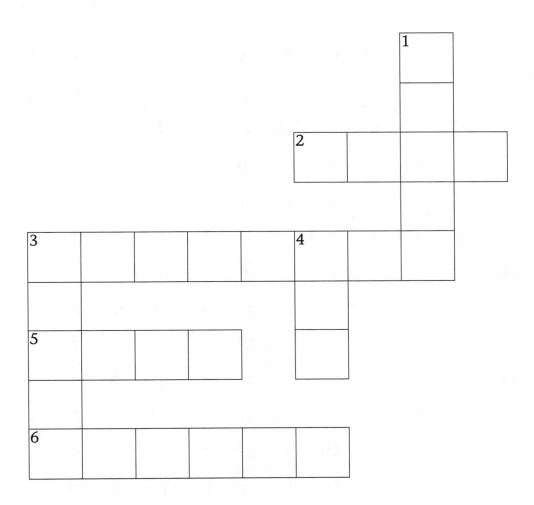

Directions: Transcribe the following words:

Across:

2. sugar
3. breakfast
5. coffee
6. napkin

Down:

1. yogurt
3. bacon
4. eggs

SPICE UP YOUR LIFE

Word Search #2   Answers in Appendix B

g	u	o	t	aɪ	m	b	k	ʌ	v	l	ɛ	k	t
k	ɔ	v	i	r	n	ʌ	t	m	ɛ	g	n	g	d
e	ʌ	d	ð	ɝ	ɝ	w	z	s	f	j	ɔ	t	ʃ
p	k	ɛ	k	i	k	ju	m	ɪ	n	h	ʒ	ɝ	o
ɚ	w	s	ɚ	ʌ	æ	ə	ɔ	h	l	e	h	m	ɛ
z	i	o	l	t	k	f	u	d	o	ɛ	m	ɚ	ɚ
e	k	ɛ	r	o	w	e	r	ɪ	t	ð	ɪ	ɪ	ʌ
h	s	r	æ	r	k	d	k	l	p	p	o	k	θ
k	f	t	k	ɛ	ɛ	v	m	t	r	t	l	p	n
r	k	m	d	g	r	k	ɔ	r	i	æ	n	d	ɚ
g	ɝ	æ	v	ə	t	r	o	ŋ	h	ɪ	t	b	m
b	i	ð	r	n	θ	p	æ	p	r	i	k	ə	g
o	ɪ	ɛ	k	o	g	t	n	ð	e	ʒ	æ	v	r
w	n	k	l	o	v	z	h	e	v	d	ɛ	g	j
f	tʃ	z	i	u	n	t	ɛ	r	ə	g	a	n	ə
k	ɑ	r	d	ə	m	ə	m	ɛ	n	æ	t	ʃ	t

Directions: Find and circle the words listed below which contain the /t/d/k/ or /g/ phonemes.

caraway	turmeric	cumin	dill
cardamom	capers	oregano	coriander
curry	paprika	nutmeg	tarragon
thyme	cloves		

Stop-Consonant

Transcription Exercise 4–15
/ p / b / t / d / k / g /

 Track: (CD 1, Track 19)
Phoneme Study Cards: 1–6

1. perpetrate _____

2. bucket _____

3. claypot _____

4. dropped _____

5. Pope _____

6. dot-to-dot _____

7. cupcake _____

8. babied _____

9. deadbolt _____

10. coat _____

11. pagoda _____

12. birdbeak _____

13. fixed _____

14. laptop _____

15. gabby _____

16. dogtag _____

17. backup _____

18. toga _____

19. pocketbook _____

20. kept _____

CHAPTER

5

Consonants: Nasals and Syllabics

Nasal Consonants

The nasal consonants are /m/n/ŋ/. They are the only consonants produced with nasal resonance. The velum is lowered, opening the velopharyngeal port to allow the breathstream to enter the nasal cavity.

Each nasal consonant is produced by a different tongue position. Tongue position is irrelevant for the /m/ as this sound is formed by closure of the lips. The /n/ is produced with lingua-alveolar contact. The /ŋ/ is formed by the back portion of the tongue contacting the velum.

/m/

Transcription Exercise 5–1   **Track: (CD 1, Track 20)**

		I	M	F
1.	mermaid			
2.	Dime			
3.	Palm			
4.	Mum			
5.	chasm			
6.	minimum			
7.	membrane			
8.	hammer			
9.	squirm			
10.	empire			

Transcription Exercise 5–2
Consonant: /m/

 Track: (CD 1, Track 21)
Refer to Study Card: 19

Phonetic Symbol	Target Word	Transcription
/m/	1. might	
	2. lamp	
	3. meat	
	4. team	
	5. camera	
	6. malt	
	7. random	
	8. harm	
	9. smell	

/m/

Distinctive Features	Tongue Position
Bilabial Nasal Voiced, front, labial, sonorant, noncontinuant, nonsibilant, nasal /m/ → (diagram) open velopharyngeal port	Tongue is flat in the oral cavity or is in place for the following phoneme. Lips are closed.

Voicing/Velopharyngeal Port	Spelling Variations
Voiced—vocal folds *adducted*. VP port is open—airflow through nasal cavity.	mm as in su*mm*er is transcribed with a single /m/. gm with silent /g/ as in diaphra*gm* mb with silent /b/ as in nu*mb* mn with silent /n/ as in hy*mn*

Word Positions	Clinical Information
Initial, medial, and final positions in SAE	Homorganic with /p/ and /b/ (made in the same place) Considered one of the earliest phonemes to develop

/n/

Transcription Exercise 5–3   **Track: (CD 1, Track 22)**

		I	M	F
1.	knapsack			
2.	kennel			
3.	nonsense			
4.	zone			
5.	prank			
6.	pneumatic			
7.	noon			
8.	gnome			
9.	beginner			
10.	seventeen			

Transcription Exercise 5–4
Consonant: /n/

 Track: (CD 1, Track 23)
Refer to Study Card: 20

Phonetic Symbol	Target Word	Transcription
/n/	1. tennis	
	2. cabin	
	3. noisy	
	4. canary	
	5. nautical	
	6. violin	
	7. handy	
	8. panel	
	9. nylon	

/n/

Distinctive Features	Tongue Position
Lingua-alveolar nasal consonant Voiced, front, nonlabial, sonorant, noncontinuant, nonsibilant, nasal /n/→ open velopharyngeal port	Tip of tongue touches the alveolar ridge. Sides of tongue touch upper molars. Back of tongue is down. Teeth and lips are open.
Voicing/Velopharyngeal Port	**Spelling Variations**
Voiced—vocal folds *ad*ducted. VP port is open—airflow through nasal cavity.	nn as in i*nn* transcribed with a single /n/ mn silent /m/ as in *mn*emonic pn silent /p/ as in *pn*eumonia kn silent /k/ as in *kn*ee gn silent /g/ as in si*gn*
Word Positions	**Clinical Information**
Initial, medial, and final positions in SAE	Homorganic with /t/ and /d/ (made in the same place)

TAKE TIME TO SMELL THE FLOWERS

Word Search #3   Answers in Appendix B

```
m  e  m  æ  g  n  o  l  j  ə  l  n
d  o  ə  p  k  dʒ ɝ  i  e  ɪ  z  ɛ
ɛ  f  o  r  dʒ u  ʌ  p  ɛ  u  ŋ  r
l  r  ð  ɪ  n  n  s  i  ɪ  o  p  v
f  s  m  m  ʌ  m  t  t  u  o  æ  θ
ɪ  p  ʃ  r  j  v  ks u  ʊ  ɝ  n  g
n  b  t  o  d  f  k  n  b  ɚ  z  o
i  t  ɪ  z  e  p  ɑ  i  i  ə  i  k
ə  d  s  o  m  ɛ  r  ə  g  o  l  d
m  k  r  p  i  o  n  i  o  ʌ  s  h
ə  g  ʊ  z  tʃ w  e  ʒ  n  k  s  ʒ
dʒ æ  z  m  i  n  ʃ  z  i  g  z  z
j  w  ɔ  ɪ  æ  n  ə  e  ə  s  r  v
ʌ  z  ɪ  n  i  ə  n  w  o  z  w  f
```

Directions: Find and circle the words listed below which contain the /m/ or /n/ phonemes.

mum   petunia   primrose
carnation   jasmine   zinnia
delphinium   magnolia   pansy
peony   begonia   marigold

/ŋ/

Transcription. Exercise 5–5　　　　　　　　**Track: (CD 1, Track 24)**

		I	M	F
1.	monkey			
2.	singing			
3.	kingdom			
4.	arrange			
5.	elongate			
6.	wrong			
7.	jingle			
8.	length			
9.	fangs			
10.	sponge			

Transcription Exercise 5–6
Consonant: /ŋ/

 Track: (CD 1, Track 25)
Refer to Study Card: 21

Reminder: Use /ɪ/ before "ing" words. See page 66

Phonetic Symbol	Target Word	Transcription
/ŋ/	1. bongo	
	2. strongly	
	3. Hong Kong	
	4. wing	
	5. tongue	
	6. shingle	
	7. dining	
	8. fang	
	9. savings	

/ŋ/

Distinctive Features	Tongue Position
Lingua-velar nasal consonant Voiced, back, nonlabial, sonorant, noncontinuant, nonsibilant, nasal 	Back of tongue is raised to contact velum. Sides of back of tongue contact back molars. Tongue tip rests just behind upper front teeth on alveolar ridge. Teeth and lips are open. Voice is directed through open VP port to nasal cavity.

Voicing/Velopharyngeal Port	Spelling Variations
Voiced—vocal folds adducted. VP port is open—airflow through nasal cavity.	Occurs as ng in words n (k) appears in mink [mɪŋk] or sink. In the same syllable and often in adjoining syllables as in income [ɪŋkʌm]. ng as in single [sɪŋəl] ngue as in tongue [tʌŋ]

Word Positions	Clinical Information
Medial and final positions in SAE	Homorganic with /k/ and /g/ (made in the same place)

Why Use The /ɪ/ Before /ŋ/?

The high front vowel /ɪ/ is used to transcribe "ing" as in "making" [mekɪŋ] or "thing" [θɪŋ].

You may have the temptation to use the [i] before /ŋ/, but resist! Compare the difference between the sound of /i/ in "meat" [mit] or "three" [θri] to the /i/ in [iŋ] and you will hear that the vowel does not sound the same.

Another important consideration is the *phonetic environment* of the high front vowel when it is adjacent to a nasal sound. Phonetic environment is defined as the phonemes which surround a specific speech sound. The /ŋ/ is a nasal consonant which requires nasal resonance through opening of the velopharyngeal port. Since the "i" gains nasal resonance, it can also cause it to sound more like /ɪ/ rather than /i/.

Remember that this rule only applies to "i-ng" orthographically and not to any other vowels before "ng" as in "sang" [sæŋ] or "strong" [strɑŋ].

NASALS

Word Search # 4   Answers in Appendix B

ʃ	d	l	ɔ	p	n	b	ʌ	dʒ	ʃ	ɪ	r	ʒ
æ	ŋ	k	ɚ	r	k	z	æ	ɝ	j	ɝ	ɛ	o
d	s	d	ʒ	t	θ	tʃ	ɪ	d	ɔ	d	k	ə
ɪ	ɑ	n	ɝ	c	ʌ	r	m	r	h	ɝ	t	k
k	j	æ	ŋ	k	ɪ	ŋ	b	ɪ	ə	s	æ	b
d	t	k	d	l	ŋ	t	s	ŋ	o	l	ŋ	ɪ
ɪ	m	m	ʃ	ə	s	i	ɪ	k	ə	b	g	e
s	l	ɪ	ŋ	g	ɚ	m	tʃ	ə	i	z	ə	w
ŋ	k	ə	w	n	z	w	ʃ	e	tʃ	d	l	i
ʃ	l	ɪ	n	i	k	m	ʌ	ŋ	k	n	ð	æ
l	ɛ	h	ð	l	o	d	r	l	ɛ	s	t	t
ʃ	ŋ	l	o	ɪ	l	æ	e	e	o	d	ɛ	l
æ	k	m	tʃ	ŋ	g	b	s	w	ɪ	ŋ	z	i
p	θ	r	z	k	n	θ	ɪ	i	u	tʃ	d	z
h	ɪ	s	s	ʒ	s	r	ŋ	m	n	r	k	ɪ

Directions: Find and circle the words listed below which contain the /ŋ/.

linger	monk
length	racing
swings	rectangle
link	anchor
drink	yanking

Crossword Puzzle for /m/, /n/, and /ŋ/
Answers in Appendix B

Directions: Transcribe the following words:

Across:
1. nine
3. kingdom
4. pneumonia

Down:
1. napkin
2. steam

Syllabics

In its simplest form, a syllabic is a consonant with a vowel-like quality. A syllabic consonant acts like a vowel. For example, the word "hidden" can be pronounced in two ways: (a) [hɪdən] or (b) [hɪdn̩]. In the first example, the tongue leaves the alveolar ridge after producing /d/ to produce the mid-central schwa vowel, and then returns to the alveolar ridge to produce /n/. In the second example, the tongue remains on the alveolar ridge after production of /d/ to produce the following syllabic /n̩/.

Use of syllabics occurs in conversational speech and in producing the words in isolation. When a word is said in isolation, the /m̩/ and /n̩/ syllabics share a homorganic (made in the same place of articulation) relationship with the previous phoneme. For example, the syllabic /m̩/ will follow /b/ and /p/ and the syllabic /n̩/ will follow /t/d/s/z/. The syllabic /l̩/ can follow any consonant. Examples of these syllabics:

Syllabic /m/	open	[opm̩]
	cabin	[kæbm̩]
	ribbon	[rɪbm̩]
Syllabic /n/	reason	[rizn̩]
	lesson	[lɛsn̩]
	ridden	[rɪdn̩]
Syllabic /l/	medal	[mɛdl̩]
	camel	[kæml̩]
	people	[pipl̩]

Transcription Exercise 5–7
Nasal Consonants / m / n / ŋ /

Track: (CD 1, Track 26)
Phoneme Study Cards: 19–21

1. nasal _____

2. monumental _____

3. among _____

4. remnant _____

5. nominate _____

6. feminine _____

7. lemonade _____

8. morning _____

9. chimney _____

10. meeting _____

11. containing _____

12. mingling _____

13. membrane _____

14. money _____

15. nanny _____

16. meringue _____

17. mountain _____

18. numerical _____

19. cinnamon _____

20. moonbeam _____

6

Consonants: Sibilants and Fricatives

Fricatives:
/s/z/f/v/ʃ/ʒ/θ/ð/h/hw/

As discussed in Chapter 3, fricatives are produced when the breathstream passes through a narrow constriction in the vocal tract. Each fricative has a voiced cognate. The /h/ and /hw/ are classified as fricatives but are not considered cognates as both phonemes are unvoiced when produced in isolation. Unlike the oral cavity, which is the source of friction for the majority of the fricatives, the glottis serves as the source of friction for the /h/ and /hw/.

/f/

Transcription Exercise 6–1   Track: (CD 1, Track 27)

		I	M	F
1.	phosphorus			
2.	pamphlet			
3.	giraffe			
4.	photo			
5.	fifteen			
6.	Joseph			
7.	spherical			
8.	monograph			
9.	fluffy			
10.	phonograph			

Transcription Exercise 6–2
Consonant: /f/

 Track: (CD 1, Track 28)
Refer to Study Card: 9

Phonetic Symbol	Target Word	Transcription
/f/	1. fun	
	2. before	
	3. fifteen	
	4. frost	
	5. coffee	
	6. leaf	
	7. laugh	
	8. float	
	9. if	

/f/

Distinctive Features	Tongue Position
Labio-dental fricative Unvoiced, front, labial, nonsonorant, continuant, nonsibilant, non-nasal /f/→	Inner border of lower lip is raised to contact upper incisors. Breathstream is continuously emitted between teeth and lower lip. Tongue position is irrelevant; may be in position for following phoneme.

Voicing/Velopharyngeal Port	Spelling Variations
Voiceless—vocal folds *ab*duct. VP port is closed.	ff is transcribed as single /f/ as in coffee. ph *ph*one, pro*ph*et gh rou*gh*, lau*gh*

Word Positions	Clinical Information
Initial, medial, and final positions in SAE	Common articulatory substitutions: p/f, b/f Cognate of /v/

/v/

Transcription Exercise 6–3   **Track: (CD 1, Track 29)**

		I	M	F
1.	vindictive			
2.	wife			
3.	chevron			
4.	weaver			
5.	of			
6.	lifesaving			
7.	never			
8.	wives			
9.	verify			
10.	stove			

Transcription Exercise 6–4
Consonant: /v/

 Track: (CD 1, Track 30)
Refer to Study Card: 10

Phonetic Symbol	Target Word	Transcription
/v/	1. vine	
	2. velvet	
	3. over	
	4. very	
	5. invite	
	6. live	
	7. value	
	8. weaver	
	9. move	

/v/

Distinctive Features	Tongue Position
Labio-dental fricative Voiced front, labial, nonsonorant, continuant, nonsibilant, non-nasal /v/→	See /f/

Voicing/Velopharyngeal Port	Spelling Variations
Voiced—vocal folds *ad*duct. VP port is closed.	ph Ste*ph*en lv silent /l/ as in ca*l*ves, sa*l*ves

Word Positions	Clinical Information
Initial, medial, and final positions in SAE	Substituted with /b/ or omitted Cognate of /f/

Crossword Puzzle for /f/ and /v/

See Answers in Appendix B

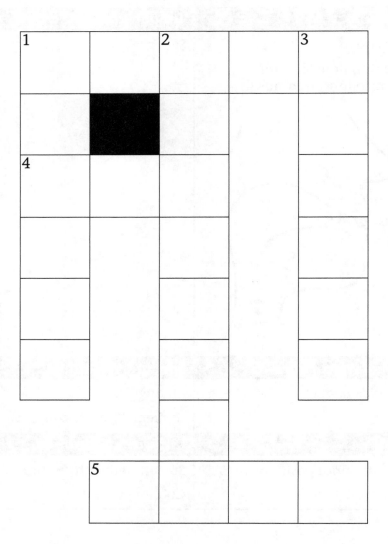

Directions: Transcribe the following words:

Across:

1. caffeine
4. vase
5. flip

Down:

1. cavity
2. festival
3. notify

MONDAY NIGHT FOOTBALL

Word Search # 5   Answers in Appendix B

v	ɪ	k	t	ɔ	r	i	h	e	d	ɪ	n
m	h	ɛ	g	d	e	t	r	r	b	s	h
ɑ	r	r	ɪ	t	ɚ	m	ɛ	i	n	k	ɛ
r	ɛ	ə	v	ɪ	n	s	k	s	ɑ	k	p
s	f	ʊ	t	b	ɔ	l	i	i	l	ɪ	d
u	ɚ	n	d	h	ɑ	r	v	v	i	k	ə
n	i	ə	s	e	f	t	i	ɚ	t	ɔ	h
b	l	u	d	w	ɪ	i	v	g	u	f	æ
f	ʊ	l	b	æ	k	l	ɑ	m	p	r	f
r	w	f	ɑ	d	s	w	r	θ	ɛ	e	b
ʊ	u	i	dʒ	d	ə	ʃ	s	ɛ	r	n	æ
k	d	l	u	æ	m	æ	ɪ	r	i	i	k
s	b	d	l	i	t	m	t	i	dʒ	ɛ	r
ɔ	f	ɛ	n	s	ɑ	d	i	f	ɛ	n	s

Directions: Find and circle the words listed below which contain the /f/ or /v/ phonemes.

referee	kickoff	fullback
football	varsity	field
victory	receiver	defense
safety	halfback	offense

/s/

Transcription Exercise 6–5   **Track: (CD1, Track 31)**

		I	M	F
1.	city			
2.	shaves			
3.	deceptive			
4.	blintz			
5.	usual			
6.	axes			
7.	bracelet			
8.	island			
9.	pseudo			
10.	Bronx			

Transcription Exercise 6–6
Consonant: /s/

 Track: (CD 1, Track 32)
Refer to Study Card: 7

Phonetic Symbol	Target Word	Transcription
/s/	1. else	
	2. asleep	
	3. superior	
	4. basin	
	5. Easter	
	6. cedar	
	7. asks	
	8. sandal	
	9. blast	

/s/

Distinctive Features	Tongue Position
Lingua-alveolar fricative Voiceless, front, nonlabial, nonsonorant, continuant, sibilant, non-nasal 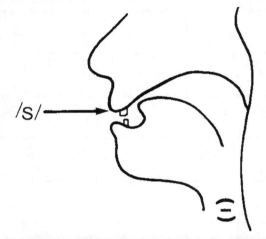	**Tongue tip up:** Tongue tip, narrowly grooved, contacts alveolar ridge behind upper incisors. Breath is continuously directed through narrow aperture between alveolar ridge and grooved tongue tip, creating turbulence. **Tongue tip down:** Tip of tongue contacts *lower* incisors near alveolar ridge. Front of tongue, slightly grooved, is raised toward alveolar ridge and forms a narrow aperture through which breath is continuously directed against front teeth, creating turbulence. Lips are apart and neutral; may be in position for following vowel.
Voicing/Velopharyngeal Port	**Spelling Variations**
Voiceless—vocal folds *ab*duct. VP port is closed.	Variable spelling Pronounced as /z/ in bu*s*iness, /ʒ/ in trea*s*ure, /ʃ/ as in *s*ure x /ks/ as in wa*x*, fi*x* c as /s/ sound in *c*ity, *c*ycle sc *sc*epter, *sc*ene st with silent /t/ as in gli*st*en, tre*st*le ps silent /p/ as in *p*sychology s as plural form, present tense, or possessive, after voiceless consonant as in cape*s*, sit*s*, Pat'*s*
Word Position	**Clinical Information**
Initial, medial, and final positions in SAE	This phoneme is frequently misarticulated. One of the most frequently occurring consonants in SAE Common substitutions include /t/ /d/ or /ʃ/. Interdental lisp: substituted with /θ/ (tip of tongue protrudes between teeth) Lateral lisp: airflow *around* tongue rather than through front of oral cavity Cognate of /z/

/z/

Transcription Exercise 6–7   **Track: (CD 1, Track 33)**

		I	M	F
1.	kids			
2.	czar			
3.	cheese			
4.	observe			
5.	business			
6.	nasal			
7.	present			
8.	is			
9.	seizure			
10.	bobsleds			

Transcription Exercise 6–8
Consonant: /z/

 Track: (CD 1, Track 34)
Refer to Study Card: 8

Phonetic Symbol	Target Word	Transcription
/z/	1. busy	
	2. visit	
	3. zircon	
	4. weasel	
	5. seas	
	6. zinnia	
	7. those	
	8. zucchini	
	9. gives	

/z/

Distinctive Features	Tongue Position
Lingua-alveolar fricative Voiced, front, nonlabial, nonsonorant, continuant, sibilant, non-nasal /z/ →	See /s/

Voicing/Velopharyngeal Port	Spelling Variations
Voiced—vocal folds *ad*duct. VP port is closed.	s as in hi*s*, wa*s*, de*s*ign, scissor*s* es plural forms or possessive as in kiss*es*, boy'*s* ss occurs as /z/ in sci*ss*ors sth a*sth*ma x *x*ylophone x forms /gz/ in e*x*amine [ɛgzæmɪn]

Word Position	Clinical Information
Initial, medial, and final positions in SAE	Commonly substituted with /d/ or /t/ Cognate of /s/

CAN YOU HEAR THE DIFFERENCE BETWEEN /s/ AND /z/?

It is not always easy to hear the difference between /s/ and /z/, especially in the final positions of words. Say the following words which all contain the /z/ as the final sound.

1. phase	16. news
2. cheese	17. sees
3. surprise	18. pies
4. fleas	19. rituals
5. tease	20. bruise
6. was	21. Eloise
7. tragedies	22. joys
8. wise	23. cardinals
9. rose	24. Japanese
10. bananas	25. is
11. cruise	26. tomatoes
12. eyes	27. skis
13. glows	28. kneels
14. choose	29. stereos
15. goes	30. advertise

Crossword Puzzle for /s/ and /z/

Answers in Appendix B

Across:

3. zip
4. sizzle
5. soldier

Down:

1. soups
2. zeal
3. Zorro
5. seasons

THE CENTER RING

Word Search #6   Answers in Appendix B

```
æ   h   m   s   t   o   ɑ   g   ɪ   t   m   k
k   æ   ɛ   l   ə   f   ɪ   n   t   s   z   ɑ
r   m   t   i   ɚ   r   h   d   r   k   ɛ   s
o   h   p   s   ɛ   ks  aɪ  t   m   ɛ   n   t
b   u   ɛ   ə   m   i   d   r   ɛ   o   tʃ  u
æ   t   r   m   ɛ   ə   h   æ   k   r   ə   m
t   b   i   s   m   l   aʊ  p   i   n   i   z
s   ɝ   k   ə   s   d   r   i   t   p   ɑ   l
j   ɑ   h   ɪ   k   e   g   z   i   b   r   ə
h   ð   æ   r   l   l   e   e   u   o   k   ɑ
u   k   l   k   aʊ  e   t   aɪ  g   ɚ   z   r
p   æ   o   n   n   b   d   dʒ  d   t   o   z
s   t   w   l   z   n   ɔ   ɝ   i   e   t   i
s   l   aɪ  ə   n   z   r   t   ɛ   n   t   s
```

Directions: Find and circle the words listed below which contain the /s/ or /z/ phonemes.

circus	clowns	acrobats
trapeze	zebra	lions
costumes	excitement	elephants
tigers	hoops	tents

Transcription Exercise 6–9
Fricative Consonants: / f / v / s / z /

 Track: (CD 1, Track 35)
Phoneme Study Cards: 7–10

1. festive _____

2. Swiss _____

3. vessel _____

4. fanciful _____

5. measles _____

6. zest _____

7. vivid _____

8. expensive _____

9. businesses _____

10. forgive _____

11. soapsuds _____

12. fasten _____

13. squeeze _____

14. scissors _____

15. pharmacy _____

16. Stephen _____

17. vice _____

18. Switzerland _____

19. safety _____

20. civilian _____

/θ/

Transcription Exercise 6–10   **Track: (CD 1, Track 36)**

		I	M	F
1.	enthusiast			
2.	Thursday			
3.	thither			
4.	Elizabeth			
5.	thirty-third			
6.	Gothic			
7.	cathedral			
8.	through			
9.	anesthesia			
10.	zenith			

Transcription Exercise 6–11
Consonant: /θ/

 Track: (CD 1, Track 37)
Refer to Study Card: 11

Phonetic Symbol	Target Word	Transcription
/θ/	1. thin	
	2. birthday	
	3. width	
	4. teeth	
	5. throw	
	6. anything	
	7. north	
	8. nothing	
	9. thaw	

/θ/

Distinctive Features	Tongue Position
Interdental fricative Voiceless, front, nonlabial, nonsonorant, continuant, nonsibilant, non-nasal /θ/ ⟶	Sides of tongue are against molars. Tip and blade of tongue are spread wide and thin in space between teeth. Breath is continuously emitted between front teeth. Lips are apart and neutral.

Voicing/Velopharyngeal Port	Spelling Variations
Voiceless—vocal folds *ab*duct. VP port is closed.	th is the only spelling th ba*th*, mon*th* th some*th*ing, au*th*or thr *th*ree

Word Positions	Clinical Information
Initial, medial, and final positions in SAE	Also known as "theta" A sound unique to the English language Commonly substituted with /t/s/f/ and /d/ Cognate of /ð/

/ð/

Transcription Exercise 6–12   **Track: (CD 1, Track 38)**

		I	M	F
1.	them			
2.	clothe			
3.	Heather			
4.	rhythm			
5.	teeth			
6.	north			
7.	whether			
8.	thigh			
9.	northern			
10.	weather			

Transcription Exercise 6–13
Consonant: /ð/

 Track: (CD 1, Track 39)
Refer to Study Card: 12

Phonetic Symbol	Target Word	Transcription
/ð/	1. this	
	2. either	
	3. there	
	4. father	
	5. seethe	
	6. though	
	7. mother	
	8. teethe	
	9. smooth	

/ð/

Distinctive Features	Tongue Position
Interdental fricative Voiced front, nonlabial, nonsonorant, continuant, nonsibilant, non-nasal /ð/ ⟶	Same tongue position as for /θ/

Voicing/Velopharyngeal Port	Spelling Variations
Voiced—vocal folds *ad*ducted. VP port is closed.	th is the only spelling th occurs in frequently used words such as *the, this, that, they, them, then, these, there, those* th ba*the*, soo*the*, bo*ther*, fea*ther*

Word Positions	Clinical Information
Initial, medial, and final positions in SAE	A sound unique to the English language Commonly substituted by /d/ and /t/ Cognate of /θ/

Transcription Exercise 6–14 **Track: (CD 1, Track 40)**

It is often difficult for beginning phonetics students to hear the difference between the voiced "th" /ð/ and unvoiced "th"/θ/. It can be helpful if you say words with these phonemes to "feel" the difference. When you pronounce the voiced "th," you will feel a vibration produced by the tongue placement between the central incisors. In addition, the vocal folds vibrate. Contrast this production with the unvoiced "th" in which there is no vocal fold vibration. Directions: Say each word and write the symbol for the voiced /ð/ or unvoiced /θ/ phoneme. Listen to the CD if you need help.

1. wreathe (verb)
2. than
3. earthworm
4. bath
5. ungathered
6. seethe
7. stethoscope
8. blithe
9. amethyst
10. featherbed
11. weatherman
12. locksmith
13. with
14. though
15. either

16. thank
17. although
18. thou
19. rhythm
20. pathway
21. Judith
22. healthy
23. marathon
24. together
25. thump
26. Southerner
27. these
28. either
29. lather
30. Keith

Crossword Puzzle for /θ/ and /ð/

Answers in Appendix B

Directions: Transcribe the following words:

Across:
1. father
2. those
3. mothers
4. thin
6. rhythm

Down:
1. feathers
3. methodic
5. north

INTERDENTAL FRICATIVE

Word Search #7   Answers in Appendix B

```
g   t   k   ɛ   l   v   b   ʌ   k   b   m   s
ɝ   ʒ   p   æ   θ   h   e   b   m   ɛ   θ   aʊ
k   p   o   r   ɛ   e   ð   ɛ   ɪ   d   ð   d
l   p   θ   t   m   v   m   ɛ   o   e   æ   m
o   o   r   æ   ð   b   ɑ   ð   ɚ   l   n   ɑ
ð   k   ɛ   n   p   f   θ   l   d   t   t   m
e   θ   d   d   ə   n   ə   ð   ɚ   p   æ   æ
v   n   k   m   g   tʃ  æ   t   ə   k   n   θ
æ   ɚ   ð   g   r   θ   ɪ   ŋ   l   l   r   ɪ
θ   n   t   æ   ɝ   ɝ   θ   ɚ   z   ɑ   t   ɛ
r   g   n   ð   v   d   r   w   ɪ   θ   aʊ  t
j   b   o   ɚ   k   h   ɪ   b   s   e   t   i
ə   æ   g   m   s   aʊ  θ   ɑ   l   m   ɛ   g
t   θ   t   θ   p   z   n   r   i   æ   n   k
```

Directions: Find and circle the words listed below which contain the /θ/ or /ð/ phonemes.

thread	moth	than	cloth
third	without	bother	clothe
thing	math	bath	path
south	another	bathe	gather

Transcription Exercise 6–15
Interdental Consonants: / θ / ð /

 Track: (CD 1, Track 41)
Phoneme Study Cards: 11–12

1. bike-a-thon _____

2. Wadsworth _____

3. southeastern _____

4. arithmetic _____

5. seventeenth _____

6. threaten _____

7. undergrowth _____

8. southernmost _____

9. Thunderbird _____

10. Plymouth _____

11. ruthlessly _____

12. Witherspoon _____

13. heartthrob _____

14. worthy _____

15. thriving _____

16. another _____

17. methodic _____

18. thoughtless _____

19. hundredth _____

20. leather _____

/h/

Transcription Exercise 6–16　　　　　　　　　Track: (CD 1, Track 42)

		I	M	F
1.	whom			
2.	rehearse			
3.	hitchhike			
4.	unwholesome			
5.	Jose			
6.	inhale			
7.	gila monster			
8.	habitat			
9.	mahogany			
10.	exhalation			

Transcription Exercise 6–17
Consonant: /h/

 Track: (CD 1, Track 43)
Refer to Study Card: 15

Phonetic Symbol	Target Word	Transcription
/h/	1. heft	
	2. harbor	
	3. mohair	
	4. uphill	
	5. hum	
	6. inherit	
	7. rehearse	
	8. hermit	
	9. unhook	

/h/

Distinctive Features	Tongue Position
Glottal fricative Voiceless, back, nonlabial, nonsonorant, continuant, nonsibilant, non-nasal ← /h/	No consistent articulatory pattern—tongue is in position for following phoneme. Breath is directed through the oral cavity.

Voicing/Velopharyngeal Port	Spelling Variations
If produced in isolation, /h/ is voiceless—vocal folds are *ab*ducted. VP port is closed.	wh *whom, whole* gh silent as in Hu*gh* h silent in *honor, honest*

Word Positions	Clinical Information
Initial and medial positions in SAE	May be replaced with glottal stop in certain dialects

/hw/ or /ʍ/

Transcription. Exercise 6–18   **Track: (CD 1, Track 44)**

		I	M	F
1.	wheel			
2.	queen			
3.	swear			
4.	why			
5.	suede			
6.	where			
7.	wholewheat			
8.	wear			
9.	wagon			
10.	square			

Transcription Exercise 6–19
Consonant: /hw/ also /ʍ/

 Track: (CD 1, Track 45)
Refer to Study Card: 16

Phonetic Symbol	Target Word	Transcription
/hw/	1. whim	
	2. overwhelm	
	3. whip	
	4. twenty	
	5. schwa	
	6. white	
	7. somewhere	
	8. whether	
	9. wharf	

/hw/ or /ʍ/

Distinctive Features	Tongue Position
Labial-velar (bilabial) fricative Voiceless, nonsibilant, continuant /hw/	Back of tongue may be raised toward soft palate, or may be in low back position for /h/. Lips may be rounded. Breath is directed through oral cavity and lip opening.
Voicing/Velopharyngeal Port	**Spelling Variations**
Voiceless; however, vocal folds *add*uct slightly to create turbulence. VP port is closed.	w following /s/ as in *s*wim, *s*wag; following /t/ as in *t*wig, *t*welve, and following "th" as in *th*wart, may be produced with the /ʍ/ wh *wh*eel, some*wh*ere
Word Positions	**Clinical Information**
Initial and medial positions in SAE	Also called inverted "w" Most commonly produced as /w/

Transcription Exercise 6–20
Consonants: /h/hw/

 Track: (CD 1, Track 46)
Phoneme Study Cards: 15–16

1. hedgehog _____

2. suede _____

3. whirl _____

4. whom _____

5. sway _____

6. wahoo _____

7. whine _____

8. handshake _____

9. hair _____

10. whiff _____

11. who _____

12. whammy _____

13. wholehearted _____

14. where _____

15. pinwheel _____

16. hymn _____

17. persuade _____

18. whistle _____

19. Ohio _____

20. whose _____

/ʃ/

Transcription Exercise 6–21   **Track: (CD 1, Track 47)**

		I	M	F
1.	condition			
2.	usher			
3.	tissue			
4.	brochure			
5.	chiffon			
6.	initial			
7.	treasure			
8.	licorice			
9.	creation			
10.	shoebrush			

Transcription Exercise 6–22
Consonant: /ʃ/

 Track: (CD 1, Track 48)
Refer to Study Card: 13

Phonetic Symbol	Target Word	Transcription
/ʃ/	1. shoe	
	2. mustache	
	3. ocean	
	4. insure	
	5. wish	
	6. ship	
	7. relish	
	8. shake	
	9. fashion	

/ʃ/

Distinctive Features	Articulatory Production
Lingua-palatal fricative Voiceless, back, nonsonorant, continuant, sibilant, non-nasal	Sides of tongue contact upper molars. Tip of tongue is at the lower central incisors; front of tongue raised toward hard palate. Breathstream is directed through and against slightly open front teeth with turbulence. Lips are slightly rounded and protruded, approximating position for /ʊ/.

Voicing/Velopharyngeal Port	Spelling Variations
Voiceless—vocal folds *ab*duct. VP port is closed.	s *s*ugar, in*s*urance c o*c*ean ch *ch*ic, musta*ch*e tion na*tion*, ac*tion* sc con*sc*ience chs fu*chs*ia

Word Positions	Clinical Information
Initial, medial, and final positions in SAE	Common articulatory substitution: t/ʃ, d/ʃ, s/ʃ Cognate of /ʒ/

/ʒ/

Transcription Exercise 6–23   Track: (CD 1, Track 49)

		I	M	F
1.	vision			
2.	aphasia			
3.	garage			
4.	station			
5.	treasure			
6.	Persia			
7.	closure			
8.	rouge			
9.	composure			
10.	television			

Transcription Exercise 6–24
Consonant: /ʒ/

 Track: (CD 1, Track 50)
Refer to Study Card: 14

Phonetic Symbol	Target Word	Transcription
/ʒ/	1. regime	
	2. loge	
	3. pleasure	
	4. division	
	5. usual	
	6. collision	
	7. beige	
	8. collage	
	9. casual	

/ʒ/

Distinctive Features	Tongue Position
Lingua-palatal fricative Voiced, back, nonlabial, nonsonorant, continuant, sibilant, non-nasal 	See /ʃ/

Voicing/Velopharyngeal Port	Spelling Variations
Voiced—vocal folds *ad*duct. VP port is closed.	s as in mea*s*ure, occa*s*ion g(e) bei*ge*, presti*ge* z a*z*ure, sei*z*ure

Word Positions	Clinical Information
Medial and final positions in SAE	Common articulation error is substitution of /d/, /t/ and omission Cognate of /ʃ/

Crossword Puzzle for /ʃ/ and /ʒ/

Answers in Appendix B

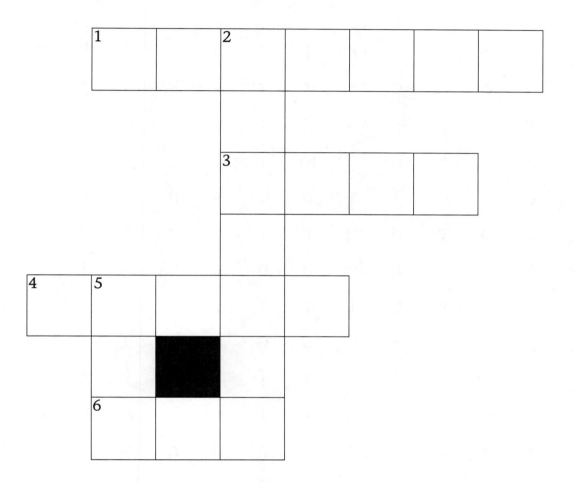

Directions: Transcribe the following words:

Across:

1. vacation
3. leisure
4. aphasia
6. shun

Down:

2. collision
5. fish

UNDER THE SEA

Word Search #8

Answers in Appendix B

```
ʃ   æ   l   o   k   ʃ   s   z   n   æ   aɪ  p
d   d   d   p   r   r   ɪ   ɪ   k   n   g   ɔ
ɪ   l   ʌ   æ   o   ɪ   t   k   θ   o   l   l
k   n   k   n   j   m   i   l   ɪ   ʃ   k   ə
d   r   m   ʃ   ɪ   p   s   s   ŋ   ə   r   n
ɪ   ɑ   ə   d   u   r   m   l   s   n   ɑ   i
s   d   ɪ   s   n   o   ə   z   z   d   f   ʒ
n   s   n   d   t   f   ɪ   ʃ   k   r   ɝ   ə
ʃ   o   l   e   θ   e   ð   ɔ   o   u   j   k
i   m   m   l   w   z   ʃ   ə   l   ʃ   æ   d
ʃ   ɑ   r   k   d   i   l   ə   h   w   b   o
l   i   s   p   r   o   n   ð   n   ɛ   r   l
æ   t   r   ɛ   ʒ   ɚ   tʃ  ɛ   s   t   t   æ
p   m   k   l   æ   m   ʃ   ɛ   l   b   m   b
h   ɪ   tʃ  u   o   d   ɔ   s   ə   s   ɚ  ɪ   ʒ
d   k   ɪ   z   b   ʌ   r   l   ɛ   m   n   r
```

Directions: Find and circle the words listed below which contain the /ʃ/ or /ʒ/ phonemes.

shrimp	treasure chest	shallow	ships
shore	crustacean	shark	fish
clamshell	ocean	shoal	shad
Polynesia			

CHAPTER

7

Consonants: Affricates /tʃ/dʒ/

The affricates are a combination of a stop-consonant immediately followed by a fricative, produced in the same breath. They are also called "stop-fricatives," which describes their manner of production. Affricates are considered obstruents as they are produced with an obstructed breathstream.

Some phoneticians prefer to write the two components of the affricates touching each other to emphasize that they are produced with a single breath impulse and to eliminate confusing the symbols with two separate phonemes.

/tʃ/

Transcription Exercise 7–1   **Track: (CD 1, Track 51)**

		I	M	F
1.	chef			
2.	hatchet			
3.	pitch			
4.	brochure			
5.	chord			
6.	culture			
7.	ache			
8.	machine			
9.	church			
10.	future			

Transcription Exercise 7–2
Consonant: /tʃ/

 Track: (CD 1, Track 52)
Refer to Study Card: 17

Phonetic Symbol	Target Word	Transcription
/tʃ/	1. chin	
	2. peaches	
	3. which	
	4. cheese	
	5. lunch	
	6. teacher	
	7. children	
	8. scotch	
	9. furniture	

/tʃ/

Distinctive Features	Tongue Position
Alveopalatal affricate Voiceless, back, nonlabial, nonsonorant, noncontinuant, sibilant, non-nasal /tʃ/	Sides of tongue against upper molars. Tip and blade of tongue close on or just behind upper alveolar ridge. Air held and compressed in oral cavity; exploded as audible breath through broad opening between alveolar ridge and front of tongue. Turbulence is created. Lips are apart and neutral.
Voicing/Velopharyngeal Port	**Spelling Variations**
Voiceless—vocal folds *abd*uct. VP port is closed.	tch ma*tch*, ca*tch* t(ure) frac*ture*, furni*ture* t(ion) men*tion*, ques*tion* nsion with intruded /t/ for /ntʃ/ as in ten*sion* [tɛntʃən] t(u) vir*tue*, na*tural* Infrequently with c as in *c*ello
Word Position	**Clinical Information**
Initial, medial, and final positions in SAE	Common articulation error of substitution of /t/ or /d/ or omitted Cognate of /dʒ/

/dʒ/

Transcription Exercise 7–3 Track: (CD 1, Track 53)

		I	M	F
1.	garage			
2.	budget			
3.	ginger			
4.	dungeon			
5.	jump			
6.	education			
7.	gesture			
8.	voyage			
9.	engine			
10.	splurge			

Transcription Exercise 7–4
Consonant: /dʒ/

 Track: (CD 1, Track 54)
Refer to Study Card: 18

Phonetic Symbol	Target Word	Transcription
/dʒ/	1. junk	
	2. enjoy	
	3. urged	
	4. vigil	
	5. wage	
	6. gem	
	7. jumbo	
	8. collagen	
	9. fudge	

/dʒ/

Distinctive Features	Tongue Position
Alveopalatal affricate Voiced, back, nonlabial, nonsonorant, noncontinuant, sibilant, non-nasal 	See /tʃ/

Voicing/Velopharyngeal Port	Spelling Variations
Voiced—vocal folds *ad*duct. VP port is closed.	gg exa*gg*erate d cor*d*ial, gra*d*ual j *j*uice, *j*erk dge e*dge* g tra*g*ic, en*g*ine, *g*ypsy dj a*dj*ust

Word Position	Clinical Information
Initial, medial, and final positions in SAE	Cognate of /tʃ/

Crossword Puzzle for /tʃ/ and /dʒ/

Answers in Appendix B

Directions: Transcribe the following words:

Across:
2. angels
3. rejoice
5. preachers

Down:
1. clergy
4. psalms

AFFRICATE

Word Search #9   Answers in Appendix B

```
k  p  ɑ  s  s  ɑ  g  e  z  e  dʒ  i  p  b  r  j  m  ɛ
n  k  w  tʃ  k  v  u  i  tʃ  kʍ  o  f  z  g  j  r  s  n
d  b  t  s  i  ə  b  ɛ  ks  tʃ  e  n  dʒ  n  u  tʃ  v  d
j  s  p  k  æ  z  h  v  s  t  o  h  i  g  m  v  ɪ  z
m  j  æ  h  u  h  ɑ  h  w  n  ɛ  w  f  dʒ  p  r  l  t
p  æ  d  v  ɛ  n  tʃ  ɚ  k  θ  u  p  ʌ  z  s  p  ɪ  m
m  e  ɔ  z  v  l  ɝ  p  æ  s  ɪ  dʒ  ɛ  p  o  k  dʒ  n
m  m  s  h  p  b  f  o  g  s  t  ʃ  dʒ  h  w  g  g  ŋ
g  ɑ  dʒ  ɪ  ŋ  k  s  s  t  z  æ  l  ɪ  o  e  æ  ʌ  ɑ
t  v  ɪ  f  k  g  θ  ɔ  d  ʃ  l  k  ʊ  j  h  s  u  ʍ
v  d  l  i  æ  o  n  d  dʒ  h  l  m  f  v  ʌ  s  ə  j
t  f  ɛ  r  ʌ  i  ʒ  r  n  ʒ  f  æ  æ  z  f  n  s  r
r  b  r  ɪ  dʒ  ɛ  z  l  ɪ  m  z  dʒ  p  ɛ  ɪ  b  z  l
j  b  w  e  ɪ  f  ŋ  ɪ  l  n  m  ɪ  v  ks  h  i  ʃ  ʌ
i  w  o  o  k  v  ɛ  ʊ  æ  ŋ  d  k  m  u  w  tʃ  h  ɛ
l  n  h  r  ʃ  ð  n  ɚ  tʃ  ɔ  o  v  h  n  j  p  ʒ  p
ʊ  z  s  ɪ  n  tʃ  ə  p  f  o  s  p  ɛ  h  t  i  tʃ  t
z  h  t  u  t  h  ʍ  b  v  u  n  ʒ  l  m  r  w  dʒ  d
```

Directions: Find and circle the words below which contain the /tʃ/ and /dʒ/ phonemes.

cheese	jinks	age	cinch
challenge	judge	adventure	village
exchange	magic	passage	
beach	bridges	teach	

Transcription Exercise 7–5
Fricative and Affricate Consonants: /ʃ/ʒ/tʃ/dʒ/

1. shoeshine   _____

2. digestion   _____

3. confusion   _____

4. entourage   _____

5. agriculture   _____

6. vivacious   _____

7. sabotage   _____

8. enchanted   _____

9. Jake   _____

10. ship-to-shore _____

11. stagecoach   _____

12. childish   _____

13. hodgepodge   _____

14. Parisian   _____

15. suggestion   _____

16. chinchilla   _____

17. collection   _____

18. fortunate   _____

19. beautician   _____

20. visualize   _____

8

Consonants: Oral Resonants /w/j/l/r/

Unlike the stop-consonants or fricatives, whose production involves full or partial obstruction of the vocal tract, the /w/j/l/ and /r/ consonants are vowel-like, as the breathstream glides smoothly through the vocal tract. The obstruction that occurs with production of this group of consonants is caused by *approximation* of the articulators. Approximation is defined as a position of closeness of the articulators, which causes some constriction. These consonants are termed *oral resonants* because they are produced in the oral cavity and gain resonance there.

/w/

Transcription Exercise 8–1   **Track: (CD 1, Track 56)**

		I	M	F
1.	once			
2.	widow			
3.	Guam			
4.	twice			
5.	iguana			
6.	where			
7.	kiwi			
8.	question			
9.	willow			
10.	anguish			

Transcription Exercise 8–2
Consonant: /w/

 Track: (CD 1, Track 57)
Refer to Study Card: 25

Phonetic Symbol	Target Word	Transcription
/w/	1. wax	
	2. jaguar	
	3. beware	
	4. swell	
	5. wonder	
	6. queen	
	7. forward	
	8. twin	
	9. wet	

/w/

Distinctive Features	Tongue Position
Bilabial lingua-palatal or lingua-velar glide Voiced, back, labial, sonorant, noncontinuant, nonsibilant, non-nasal /W/ →	High back position (as for /u/). Moves into position for following sound. Lips rounded and protruded, but may unround quickly for transition to next sound.

Voicing/Velopharyngeal Port	Spelling Variations
Voiced—vocal folds *ad*ducted. VP port is closed.	o *one*, *once*, every*o*ne w silent in *w*ho, *w*hole, s*w*ord, ans*w*er, *w*rite (ng) u /w/ glide occurs for /u/ in la*ngu*age [læŋgwɪdʒ]

Word Positions	Clinical Information
Initial and medial positions in SAE	kw represents the "q" sound as in *q*uit Can be omitted from clusters such as sw in *sw*eet

ORAL RESONANT

Word Search #10   Answers in Appendix B

g	w	ɑ	n	t	ɑ	n	ɑ	m	o	b	e
ʃ	ɛ	w	e	r	s	ð	r	d	b	ʃ	s
s	ɑ	b	s	ð	ŋ	l	r	j	o	m	h
æ	p	v	ɪ	v	o	ʃ	tʃ	b	m	n	aʊ
n	ɑ	k	v	f	w	ɑ	t	ɚ	l	u	w
w	p	r	ɪ	i	ʌ	ə	j	v	w	θ	ɪ
ɑ	w	ɝ	l	d	w	ɔ	r	w	ʌ	n	t
n	tʃ	ɪ	w	p	b	t	d	k	g	s	z
h	ɑ	b	ɔ	r	æ	p	e	p	k	w	ɚ
ɪ	ʒ	n	r	e	dʒ	ɚ	u	ɔ	o	θ	o
l	ʃ	æ	ʊ	t	b	n	z	b	l	ɑ	ð
r	w	ɛ	p	ə	n	e	w	l	d	j	ɝ
d	p	ɛ	t	e	v	i	h	b	w	e	m
p	æ	n	d	p	aʊ	w	ɚ	ʊ	ɔ	l	u
ɚ	z	d	ɔ	l	t	r	d	ʒ	r	v	i

Directions: Find and circle the words listed below which contain the /w/ phoneme.

Civil War	howitzer
World War One	Cold War
Guantanamo Bay	power
Waterloo	weapon

/j/

		I	M	F
1.	inject			
2.	royal			
3.	yet			
4.	zillion			
5.	bunion			
6.	spaniel			
7.	yoyo			
8.	layette			
9.	figure			
10.	coyote			

Transcription Exercise 8–4
Consonant: /j/

 Track: (CD 1, Track 59)
Refer to Study Card: 23

Phonetic Symbol	Target Word	Transcription
/j/	1. your	
	2. beyond	
	3. yield	
	4. papaya	
	5. yonder	
	6. familiar	
	7. yarn	
	8. billion	
	9. yes	

/j/

Distinctive Features	Tongue Position
Lingua-palatal glide Voiced, back, nonlabial, sonorant, noncontinuant, nonsibilant, non-nasal 	Tongue is in high front position approximating /i/. Ready to move into position for the next sound. Lips are apart and neutral.

Voicing/Velopharyngeal Port	Spelling Variations
Voiced—vocal folds *ad*duct. VP port is closed.	i on*i*on, Will*i*am j hallelu*j*ah l bouil*l*on /j/ is often intrusive between words ending in /i/ or /ɪ/ and those beginning with a vowel: see it [sijɪt]

Word Positions	Clinical Information
Initial and medial positions in SAE	Articulation error: substituted with /w/ or omitted

/l/

Transcription Exercise 8–5   **Track: (CD 1, Track 60)**

		I	M	F
1.	mall			
2.	linoleum			
3.	whale			
4.	apple			
5.	fellow			
6.	calves			
7.	lullaby			
8.	flotilla			
9.	helm			
10.	sociable			

Transcription Exercise 8–6
Consonant: /l/

 Track: (CD 1, Track 61)
Refer to Study Card: 22

Phonetic Symbol	Target Word	Transcription
/l/	1. lucky	
	2. lemon	
	3. clown	
	4. sandal	
	5. golden	
	6. else	
	7. bridal	
	8. flea	
	9. Leon	

/l/

Distinctive Features	Tongue Position
Lingua–alveolar lateral (liquid)	Tip of tongue and part of blade contact upper alveolar ridge.
Voiced, front, nonlabial, sonorant, noncontinuant, nonsibilant, non-nasal	Lips are apart and neutral.
	Airflow is around the sides of the tongue for lateral emission of airstream.

/l/ →

Voicing/Velopharyngeal Port	Spelling Variations
Voiced—vocal folds *ad*duct.	Appears consistently as *l*
VP port is closed.	le bott*le*, midd*le*
	el funn*el*, kenn*el*
	sl with silent *s* in ai*sl*e

Word Positions	Clinical Information
Initial, medial, and final positions in SAE	

/ɹ/

Transcription Exercise 8–7   Track: (CD 1, Track 62)

		I	M	F
1.	wrap			
2.	rye			
3.	scar			
4.	report			
5.	rubber			
6.	wardrobe			
7.	wry			
8.	garden			
9.	before			
10.	deer			

Transcription Exercise 8–8
Consonant: /r/

 Track: (CD 1, Track 63)
Refer to Study Card: 24

Phonetic Symbol	Target Word	Transcription
/r/	1. write	
	2. impress	
	3. reduce	
	4. sorry	
	5. rhyme	
	6. already	
	7. chair	
	8. rub	
	9. bar	

/r/

Distinctive Features	Tongue Position
Alveo-palatal liquid (glide) Voiced, front, labial, sonorant, noncontinuant, nonsibilant, non-nasal ← /r/	Sides of the tongue are against upper molars. Back of tongue may be slightly elevated. Tongue is raised toward hard palate just behind alveolar ridge but without contact. Lips may be slightly protruded similar to /ʊ/ but usually take the position of the surrounding vowel. If tongue tip is curled back toward palate, referred to as retroflex.

Voicing/Velopharyngeal Port	Spelling Variations
Voiced—vocal folds *ad*duct. VP port is closed.	wr *wrote, wren* rh *rhinoceros, rhyme*

Word Positions	Clinical Information
Initial, medial, and final positions in SAE	Common articulation error is substitution of w/r, especially in children under the age of 7 years.

Influence of the /r/ Sound

The /r/ phoneme can influence the vowel which precedes it. The vowels /i/ɛ/ɑ/o/ can occur with the /r/ in the same syllable as in the words "deer" [dir], "care [kɛr], "star" [stɑr], and "more" [mor].

The influence of the /r/ sound occurs especially in the vowel + r combination of /ɛr/ as in the word "hair" [hɛr]. Because of the location of the vowel adjacent to the /r/, the front of the tongue is in a lower position than would normally be expected. In this way, the tongue position makes the vowel sound of the /e/ closer to that of /ɛ/, resulting in the use of /ɛr/.

/ir/

Transcription Exercise 8–9   **Track: (CD 1, Track 64)**

		I	M	F
1.	spear			
2.	weird			
3.	series			
4.	steer			
5.	pear			
6.	fierce			
7.	era			
8.	career			
9.	mirth			
10.	wire			

/ɛr/

Transcription Exercise 8–10   **Track: (CD 1, Track 65)**

		I	M	F
1.	heir			
2.	square			
3.	barrel			
4.	ware			
5.	trailer			
6.	air			
7.	pearl			
8.	chair			
9.	bear			
10.	caramel			

/ɑr/

Transcription Exercise 8–11   Track: (CD 1, Track 66)

		I	M	F
1.	heart			
2.	star			
3.	sergeant			
4.	farce			
5.	carriage			
6.	stare			
7.	marry			
8.	marine			
9.	party			
10.	carbon			

/ɔr/

Transcription Exercise 8–12   **Track: (CD 1, Track 67)**

		I	M	F
1.	fourth			
2.	quart			
3.	parlor			
4.	wharf			
5.	soar			
6.	wart			
7.	rumor			
8.	court			
9.	pour			
10.	world			

VOWEL +r

Word Search # 11   Answers in Appendix B

t n ʒ g f o r s k o r m

k p s ʃ j s g o v f o e

e z ə ɪ ʌ j i r l i ʒ o

k n ɛ u g ɑ r d b z ɔ f

r ks o j i t θ h m θ ʊ i

ɛ r f ɛ r r d f m ɝ i r

f o r w o r n w ɑ ʌ ɪ s

b g k ɛ r w r o r n ɛ p

u s r p e ɝ i r ʃ ə ð b

l k tʃ k ɑ r f ɛ r h e t

k w j d r s z s l ɛ d d

ɛ ɛ z s n m ɑ ŋ dʒ z ɛ k

ə r z ɚ k o r t j ɑ r d

r g ʊ p o r z ʊ w o i g

Directions: Find and circle the words listed below which contain the vowel + r sounds: /ir/or/ar/ɛr/.

yearly	guard	czars	dairy	forewarn
sword	square	carfare	pours	
ear	marsh	airfare	fourscore	
gear	fierce	careworn	courtyard	

Crossword Puzzle for /j/, /l/, and /r/

Answers in Appendix B

Directions: Transcribe the following words:

Across:
2. yellow
4. rose
5. jungle green
7. violet
8. maroon

Down:
1. teal
3. orange
6. lavender

WHAT'S IN A NAME?

Word Search #12   Answers in Appendix B

r	u	θ	v	g	e	h	k	o	w	k	l
s	ə	s	ɪ	o	k	ɑ	l	i	n	m	o
ɪ	n	s	ɑ	g	n	j	u	k	r	v	r
l	r	r	ə	b	m	ŋ	i	o	ɝ	ɛ	ɛ
ɛ	ə	u	f	l	o	t	z	θ	ʌ	s	t
r	l	d	r	ə	s	ə	l	l	ɛ	o	ə
i	d	ɑ	m	t	j	o	h	æ	n	r	ɚ
s	f	f	r	ɑ	n	ə	l	d	ʃ	t	i
o	p	ks	k	d	e	r	u	ð	s	m	l
l	o	r	e	n	e	f	ə	t	s	r	e
t	t	dʒ	g	g	ʃ	o	ʊ	b	j	ɛ	n
m	ɪ	o	l	ɪ	v	i	ə	tʃ	ɛ	t	ð
r	h	r	z	ʒ	ð	ɔ	ɑ	ɪ	t	k	o
e	h	j	o	l	æ	n	d	ə	ɑ	w	ə

Directions: Find and circle the words listed below which contain the /j/, /l/, or /r/ phonemes.

Rudolph	Ronald	Ruth
Yolanda	Louise	Colleen
Russell	Johann	Elaine
Olivia	Loretta	Yetta
Lorraine	Larry	Rebecca

Transcription Exercise 8–13
Vowel + r: /or/ir/ɛr/ɑr/

 Track: (CD 1, Track 68)
Phoneme Study Cards: 44–47

1. earmark   _____

2. careworn   _____

3. ore   _____

4. spears   _____

5. carport   _____

6. sheer   _____

7. hardware   _____

8. dart   _____

9. forlorn   _____

10. rare   _____

11. sparse   _____

12. aardvark   _____

13. jeer   _____

14. bore   _____

15. foursquare   _____

16. farce   _____

17. coarse   _____

18. smears   _____

19. starch   _____

20. bear   _____

Transcription Exercise 8–14
Oral Resonant Consonants: /l/r/j/w/

 Track: (CD 1, Track 69)
Phoneme Study Cards: 22–25

1. yoke   _____

2. dwarf   _____

3. leeway   _____

4. dominion   _____

5. quibble   _____

6. larceny   _____

7. uranium   _____

8. illustrate   _____

9. rally   _____

10. Sawyer   _____

11. radiator   _____

12. quietly   _____

13. valiant   _____

14. frequency   _____

15. lawyer   _____

16. wayward   _____

17. Yolanda   _____

18. stallions   _____

19. wrestle   _____

20. yawn   _____

CHAPTER

9

Articulation of Vowels

Vowels play a very special role in our speech by forming the nucleus of a fundamental unit of phonetic structure: the *syllable*. We can define a syllable as including two major elements. These include the onset of the syllable (a consonant that releases the *nucleus* of the syllable) and the rhyme. The rhyme consists of two parts, the nucleus (the vowel itself) and the coda or consonant that may be added on the end of the vowel. For example, for the syllable /sæt/ ("sat"), the onset is the consonant /s/, and the rhyme consists of the nucleus vowel which is /æ/ plus the coda or consonant /t/. It is convenient to call the consonant /s/ the *releaser* of the nucleus vowel and /t/ the *arrester* of the nucleus vowel.

Vowels are produced with a mostly unobstructed vocal tract. In contrast to consonants, vowels are classified solely by tongue placement to describe place of articulation. Manner of articulation for vowels is similar to continuants. For voicing, all vowels are voiced.

Prominent Articulatory Vowel Positions

The vowel quadrangle (Figure 9–1) is a very useful tool to describe vowel production as it provides convenient reference points for specifying tongue position.

The position of the *highest point of the arch of the tongue* is considered to be the point of articulation of the vowel. The *vertical dimension* of the vowel quadrangle is known as vowel *height:* high, central (mid), or low. The *horizontal dimension* of the vowel quadrangle, or tongue advancement, identifies how far forward the tongue is located in the oral cavity. Vowels are also described by the tenseness or laxness of the tongue. The tense vowels are produced with additional muscle tension, while the lax vowels are produced with less tenseness of the speech musculature.

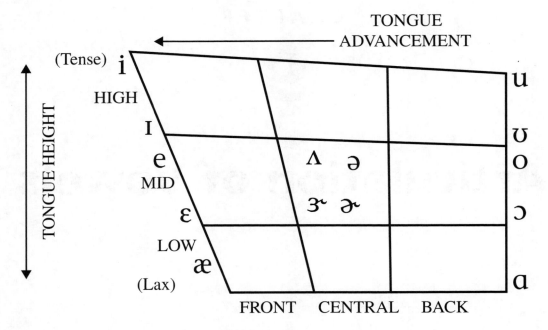

Figure 9–1. The vowel quadrangle.

CHAPTER

10

Front Vowels

As the name implies, front vowels of Standard American English are produced in the front of the oral cavity. The tongue is shifted forward to produce /i/ɪ/e/ɛ/æ/. As you say these vowels, you will note that your tongue begins at the highest point in the oral cavity and progresses downward to the lowest point. These vowels are produced with unrounded lips that may be slightly retracted.

/i/

Transcription Exercise 10–1   **Track: (CD 2, Track 1)**

		I	M	F
1.	yes			
2.	leaving			
3.	eel			
4.	thieves			
5.	people			
6.	cheapen			
7.	quiche			
8.	street			
9.	helix			
10.	hire			

Transcription Exercise 10–2
Vowel: /i/

 Track: (CD 2, Track 2)
Refer to Study Card: 26

Phonetic Symbol	Target Word	Transcription
/i/	1. eat	
	2. keep	
	3. deed	
	4. key	
	5. beak	
	6. pick	
	7. beet	
	8. tea	
	9. deep	

/i/

Distinctive Features	Tongue Position
High front tense (unrounded) vowel	Tongue moves forward and elevates toward hard palate.
	Sides of back of tongue close against upper molars.
	Front portion of tongue is raised high in oral cavity.
	Lips are parted slightly.
	Airflow is through the oral cavity.

Voicing/Velopharyngeal Port	Spelling Variations
Voiced—vocal folds *ad*duct.	e *be, me, we*
VP port is closed.	ee *feet, three*
	ea *eat, teach, east*
	ey *key*

Word Positions	Clinical Information
Initial, medial, and final positions in SAE	

/ɪ/

Transcription Exercise 10–3   **Track: (CD 2, Track 3)**

		I	M	F
1.	mild			
2.	it			
3.	pixie			
4.	billion			
5.	fine			
6.	guilt			
7.	villain			
8.	sincere			
9.	lymph			
10.	fin			

Transcription Exercise 10–4
Vowel: /ɪ/

 Track: (CD 2, Track 4)
Refer to Study Card: 27

Phonetic Symbol	Target Word	Transcription
/ɪ/	1. kick	
	2. gig	
	3. build	
	4. tick	
	5. it	
	6. bit	
	7. pick	
	8. kid	
	9. big	

/ɪ/

Distinctive Features	Tongue Position
High front lax (unrounded) vowel	Middle to front portion of tongue is raised toward hard palate and alveolar ridge.
	Sides of back of tongue close against upper molars.
	Tip of tongue touches lightly behind lower front teeth.
	Lips are apart.
	Airflow is through the oral cavity.

Voicing/Velopharyngeal Port	Spelling Variations
Voiced—vocal folds *add*uct.	i *if, in*
VP port is closed.	y *gym, hy*mn
	ee b*ee*n
	ui q*ui*z
	o w*o*men
	u b*u*sy

Word Position	Clinical Information
Initial, medial, and final positions in SAE	Referred to as the "short i"
	Many prefer to transcribe using /i/ rather than /ɪ/ in syllables that are unstressed as in "baby" [bebi]

/ɛ/

Transcription Exercise 10–5   **Track: (CD 2, Track 5)**

		I	M	F
1.	entail			
2.	penguin			
3.	bell			
4.	mild			
5.	yes			
6.	elf			
7.	gang			
8.	ethic			
9.	guess			
10.	jealous			

Transcription Exercise 10–6
Vowel: /ɛ/

 Track: (CD 2, Track 6)
Refer to Study Card: 28

Phonetic Symbol	Target Word	Transcription
/ɛ/	1. meld	
	2. end	
	3. dell	
	4. den	
	5. led	
	6. knell	
	7. dense	
	8. sled	
	9. etch	

/ɛ/

Distinctive Features	Tongue Position
Mid-front lax (unrounded) vowel	Sides of back of tongue touch against upper molars.
	Middle to front portion of tongue is raised slightly toward hard palate and alveolar ridge.
	Tip of tongue touches lightly behind lower front teeth.
	Lips are apart and neutral.
	Airflow is through the oral cavity.

Voicing/Velopharyngeal Port	Spelling Variations
Voiced—vocal folds *ad*duct.	*e* end, *ebb*, t*e*n
VP port is closed.	*ea* h*ea*d, st*ea*dy
	ai s*ai*d
	ie fr*ie*nd

Word Positions	Clinical Information
Initial and medial positions in SAE	Also known as the epsilon (from the Greek alphabet) or "short e"

/e/

Transcription Exercise 10–7　　　　　　　**Track: (CD 2, Track 7)**

		I	M	F
1.	acorn			
2.	sleigh			
3.	vein			
4.	dial			
5.	leisure			
6.	gain			
7.	bag			
8.	lei			
9.	attain			
10.	reindeer			

Transcription Exercise 10–8
Vowel: /e/

 Track: (CD 2, Track 8)
Refer to Study Card: 29

Phonetic Symbol	Target Word	Transcription
/e/	1. vase	
	2. stays	
	3. Zane	
	4. ate	
	5. faze	
	6. taste	
	7. face	
	8. shave	
	9. fate	

/e/

Distinctive Features	Tongue Position
Mid-front tense (unrounded) vowel 	Tongue is raised to mid-portion of oral cavity and shifts forward. Tip is at lower front teeth and makes contact with posterior portion of alveolar ridge; tongue contacts upper molars laterally. Lips are apart. Airflow is through the oral cavity.
Voicing/Velopharyngeal Port	**Spelling Variations**
Voiced—vocal folds *ad*duct. VP port is closed.	a *a*che et ball*et* ea *s*t*ea*k ai g*ai*t ee matin*ee*
Word Position	**Clinical Information**
Initial, medial, and final positions in SAE	Also known as the "long a" Some phoneticians use /eɪ/ to represent this sound

/æ/

Transcription Exercise 10–9 Track: (CD 2, Track 9)

		I	M	F
1.	advance			
2.	pan			
3.	ant			
4.	mall			
5.	pain			
6.	dampness			
7.	quack			
8.	cascade			
9.	math			
10.	went			

Transcription Exercise 10–10
Vowel: /æ/

 Track: (CD 2, Track 10)
Refer to Study Card: 30

Phonetic Symbol	Target Word	Transcription
/æ/	1. sash	
	2. fast	
	3. ash	
	4. staff	
	5. vat	
	6. shaft	
	7. tat	
	8. as	
	9. salve	

/æ/

Distinctive Features	Tongue Position
Low front lax (unrounded) vowel /æ/ ——→	Middle to front portion of tongue is raised toward hard palate, but is low in the mouth so that it rarely contacts upper molars. Tip of tongue is near lower front teeth. Lips are widely separated. Airflow is through the oral cavity.
Voicing/Velopharyngeal Port	**Spelling Variations**
Voiced—vocal folds *ad*duct. VP port is closed.	a *at* ai pl*ai*d ua g*ua*rantee au l*au*gh i mer*i*ngue
Word Positions	**Clinical Information**
Initial and medial positions in SAE	Also known as "short a" or "ash"

Crossword Puzzle for /i/, /ɪ/, /ɛ/, /æ/, /e/, and /w/

Answers in Appendix B

Directions: Transcribe the following words:

Across:
1. Webster
2. Winston
4. Lane
5. Mary

Down:
1. Wynn
2. William
3. Tim
6. Sheila

FOR THE BIRDS

Word Search #13   Answers in Appendix B

v g e h k g r i b o w k

f ɪ n p i k ɑ k z v m z

l i p w ʌ tʃ ɪ k ə b i ɔ

o g ɛ ʃ b ə l d f ɛ v u

t ə r o m s e ɛ g s g r

p l ə ɛ t f g n d o ə k

i ð k ɚ l æ k d v r ʃ i

r ɝ i ʌ b l u dʒ e t j w

ɛ r t θ k k dʒ s r m ɝ i

n i n n æ ə tʃ ɪ t æ ɛ s

ɔ n g m o n n ə w g ə f

ʒ e r l j h e ɛ ð p t ɪ

h i g r ɛ t z d r aɪ ŋ n

m ɪ o l ɪ t v i ə i i tʃ

Directions: Find and circle the words listed below which contain the front vowels: /i/ɪ/ɛ/æ/e/.

eagle	finch	grebe
egg	parakeet	chickadee
bluejay	egret	kiwi
wren	eaglet	peacock
falcon	canary	

Transcription Exercise 10–11
Front Vowels: /i/ɪ/ɛ/e/æ/

1. flame   _____

2. alley   _____

3. believe   _____

4. raisin   _____

5. weekday   _____

6. relax   _____

7. ask   _____

8. people   _____

9. remnant   _____

10. reign   _____

11. gymnast   _____

12. apron   _____

13. namesake   _____

14. busy   _____

15. caffeine   _____

16. women   _____

17. headache   _____

18. please   _____

19. biscuit   _____

20. eldest   _____

11

Central Vowels

The central vowels are /ə/ʌ/ɚ/ɝ/. As the name indicates, these vowels are produced in the middle portion of the oral cavity, midway between the front and back vowels. The /ə/ and /ɚ/ are classified as unstressed vowels and the /ʌ/ and /ɝ/ are produced with stress. This category of vowels usually is difficult for beginning phonetics students to master because it can be difficult to determine whether a stressed or unstressed vowel should be used.

/ə/

Transcription Exercise 11–1 Track: (CD 2, Track 12)

		I	M	F
1.	ahead			
2.	rattan			
3.	machine			
4.	baton			
5.	cabana			
6.	hello			
7.	cup			
8.	agree			
9.	buffet			
10.	cocoon			

Transcription Exercise 11–2
Vowel: /ə/

 Track: (CD 2, Track 13)
Refer to Study Card: 31

Phonetic Symbol	Target Word	Transcription
/ə/	1. galore	
	2. support	
	3. alone	
	4. compose	
	5. condone	
	6. patrol	
	7. rapport	
	8. oppose	
	9. oral	

/ə/

Distinctive Features	Tongue Position
Mid-central lax vowel (unrounded, unstressed)	Tongue is flat, but can have a slight arch; tip is at lower front teeth.
	Lips are apart and neutral.
	Airflow is through the oral cavity.

/ə/

Voicing/Velopharyngeal Port	Spelling Variations
Voiced—vocal folds *ad*duct.	There is no specific letter of the alphabet to represent the schwa. Can substitute for any vowel:
VP port is closed.	a m*a*chine u talc*u*m e r*e*port i hosp*i*tal o pr*o*found ai uncert*ai*n eo pig*eo*n

Word Positions	Clinical Information
Initial, medial, and final positions in SAE	Known as the schwa

Crossword Puzzle for /ə/

Answers in Appendix B

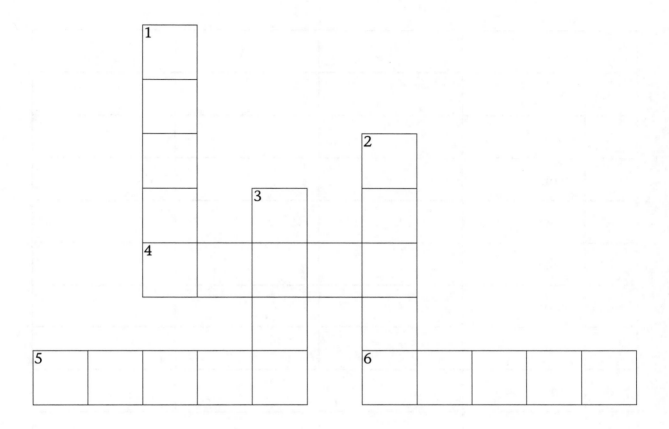

Across:

4. suppose
5. cocoon
6. lagoon

Down:

1. papoose
2. guzzle
3. upon

/ʌ/

Transcription Exercise 11–3   **Track: (CD 2, Track 14)**

		I	M	F
1.	of			
2.	chug			
3.	won			
4.	uncut			
5.	was			
6.	young			
7.	rust			
8.	up			
9.	one			
10.	roost			

Transcription Exercise 11–4
Vowel: /ʌ/

 Track: (CD 2, Track 15)
Refer to Study Card: 32

Phonetic Symbol	Target Word	Transcription
/ʌ/	1. of	
	2. touch	
	3. thumb	
	4. was	
	5. tunnel	
	6. pun	
	7. mutt	
	8. shovel	
	9. nut	

/ʌ/

Distinctive Features	Tongue Position
Mid-central vowel (unrounded, stressed)	See tongue position for schwa /ə/
	Tongue may be slightly more retracted as in production for /ɑ/.

Voicing/Velopharyngeal Port	Spelling Variations
Voiced—vocal folds *ad*duct.	u most frequent and consistent as in p*u*g, s*u*n, h*u*ndred
VP port is closed.	ou r*ou*gh, d*ou*ble
	o t*o*n, s*o*n, t*o*ngue
	oe d*oe*s
	oo bl*oo*d

Word Positions	Clinical Information
Initial and medial positions in SAE	Also referred to as the caret or inverted "v"

Crossword Puzzle for /ʌ/

Answers in Appendix B

Directions: Transcribe the following words:

Across:
3. unglued
6. shut

Down:
1. dust
2. hush
4. gumbo
5. duck

/ɚ/

Transcription Exercise 11–5   Track: (CD 2, Track 16)

		I	M	F
1.	actor			
2.	earner			
3.	nerd			
4.	sugar			
5.	anger			
6.	neighbor			
7.	creature			
8.	nature			
9.	glamour			
10.	forbid			

Transcription Exercise 11–6
Vowel: /ɚ/

 Track: (CD 2, Track 17)
Refer to Study Card: 33

Phonetic Symbol	Target Word	Transcription
/ɚ/	1. nature	
	2. major	
	3. baker	
	4. razor	
	5. later	
	6. pacer	
	7. failure	
	8. neighbor	
	9. safer	

/ɚ/

Distinctive Features	Tongue Position
Mid-central r-colored lax vowel (unstressed) ← /ɚ/	Tongue is slightly elevated from neutral position. Sides of tongue close against upper molars. Lips are apart. Airflow is through the oral cavity. Produced with same tongue position as /ɝ/ with the exception that the tongue is more relaxed and duration of this phoneme is shorter than for /ɝ/.

Voicing/Velopharyngeal Port	Spelling Variations
Voiced—vocal folds *adduct*. VP port is closed.	Most often used in unstressed positions of words er butt*er* or maj*or* our glam*our* ure meas*ure*

Word Positions	Clinical Information
Initial, medial, and final positions in SAE	Also known as the hooked schwar or unstressed schwar.

Crossword Puzzle for /ɚ/

Answers in Appendix B

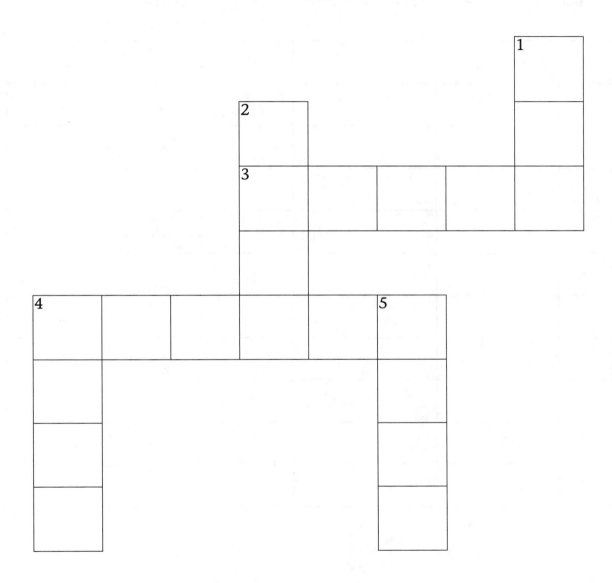

Directions: Transcribe the following words:

Across:
3. flower
4. lantern

Down:
1. ever
2. effort
4. leader
5. never

/ɝ/

Transcription Exercise 11–7 **Track: (CD 2, Track 18)**

		I	M	F
1.	herb			
2.	worst			
3.	slur			
4.	chirp			
5.	savor			
6.	urn			
7.	feature			
8.	earn			
9.	turtle			
10.	myrtle			

Transcription Exercise 11–8
Vowel: /ɝ/

 Track: (CD 2, Track 19)
Refer to Study Card: 34

Phonetic Symbol	Target Word	Transcription
/ɝ/	1. urge	
	2. verb	
	3. birth	
	4. third	
	5. dirge	
	6. burr	
	7. girth	
	8. germ	
	9. earth	

/ɝ/

Distinctive Features	Tongue Position
Mid-central r-colored tense vowel (stressed)	Tongue is slightly elevated from neutral position.
	Sides of tongue close against upper molars.
	Lips are apart.
	Airflow is through the oral cavity.

/ɝ/

Voicing/Velopharyngeal Port	Spelling Variations
Voiced—vocal folds *ad*duct.	er h*er*d, m*er*chant, f*er*n
VP port is closed.	ur *ur*ge, f*ur*, t*ur*tle
	ir ch*ir*p, b*ir*th
	ear *ear*n, p*ear*l
	or w*or*m
	our j*our*ney

Word Positions	Clinical Information
Initial, medial, and final positions in SAE	Also known as the reversed, hooked epsilon

Crossword Puzzle for /ɝ/

Answers in Appendix B

Directions: Transcribe the following words:

Across:
2. herbal
4. thirsty
6. nursemaid

Down:
1. burst
3. zircon
5. third

MID-CENTRAL VOWELS

Word Search #14   Answers in Appendix B

k	p	s	ɝ	θ	k	i	o	s	ɪ	l	v	ɚ	s
r	e	o	z	n	n	p	f	ɛ	l	b	z	ɛ	t
ɛ	ʌ	ð	p	ɛ	d	b	ɝ	t	i	w	ɝ	f	o
k	b	e	h	w	j	r	dʒ	i	d	e	dʒ	ɚ	θ
ɚ	s	h	ɝ	ɑ	p	j	z	θ	ɚ	ʌ	ʊ	t	h
d	b	ʌ	l	h	m	e	u	ɝ	ʍ	ɝ	ɛ	u	dʒ
p	s	f	i	ə	p	m	p	v	n	θ	p	ɝ	ə
n	æ	ɪ	ɚ	n	m	ɛ	d	ɚ	m	kʍ	t	ð	ʌ
d	h	n	o	dʒ	n	kʍ	t	æ	ŋ	e	t	o	h
e	ʃ	ɝ	t	v	g	s	o	n	æ	k	d	ʃ	æ
m	w	s	θ	s	t	p	h	ɑ	g	ɚ	o	g	m
m	j	p	v	t	v	ɝ	ʌ	d	ɚ	z	t	m	ɚ
g	t	i	z	o	t	s	f	n	ɛ	w	tʃ	e	h
t	v	w	ɛ	j	r	w	m	ɑ	d	ɚ	n	dʒ	o

Directions: Find and circle the words listed below which contain the /ɝ/ or /ɚ/ phonemes.

earthquake	nurse	record
urge	modern	effort
earlier	paper	hammer
purse	leader	
shirt	silver	

Transcription Exercise 11–9
Central Vowels: /ə/ʌ/ɚ/ɝ/

 Track: (CD 2, Track 20)
Phoneme Study Cards: 31–34

1. hamburger   _____

2. suds   _____

3. kern   _____

4. cover   _____

5. occur   _____

6. fervor   _____

7. undone   _____

8. eardrum   _____

9. murmur   _____

10. awhile   _____

11. turner   _____

12. confirm   _____

13. buzzer   _____

14. mature   _____

15. buffer   _____

16. chirp   _____

17. serge   _____

18. verse   _____

19. submerge   _____

20. merger   _____

12

Back Vowels

As the name indicates, the back vowels /u/ʊ/o/ɔ/ɑ/ are produced in the back portion of the oral cavity. The posterior portion of the tongue is elevated. If you say these vowels in sequence, you can feel the descent in order.

/u/

Transcription Exercise 12–1   **Track: (CD 2, Track 21)**

		I	M	F
1.	noodle			
2.	do			
3.	dew			
4.	should			
5.	ooze			
6.	suit			
7.	boutique			
8.	fool			
9.	duke			
10.	two			

Transcription Exercise 12–2
Vowel: /u/

 Track: (CD 2, Track 22)
Refer to Study Card: 35

Phonetic Symbol	Target Word	Transcription
/u/	1. rule	
	2. sue	
	3. loose	
	4. rue	
	5. loop	
	6. flew	
	7. sloop	
	8. pool	
	9. fool	

/u/

Distinctive Features	Tongue Position
High back tense rounded vowel 	Back of tongue is raised high and tense in oral cavity. Sides of back of tongue close against upper molars. Tongue tip is behind lower front teeth. Lips are rounded.
Voicing/Velopharyngeal Port	**Spelling Variations**
Voiced—vocal folds *ad*duct. VP port is closed.	Occurs most frequently as "oo" as in b*oo*t, c*oo*l, t*oo* o d*o*, wh*o* ew bl*ew*, gr*ew* ou s*ou*p, gr*ou*p ui fr*ui*t, br*ui*se R*oo*f, r*oo*t, h*oo*p can be pronounced with either /u/ or /ʊ/
Word Position	**Clinical Information**
Medial and final position in SAE	Rarely occurs in Initial position in SAE, such as "*oops*"

/ʊ/

Transcription Exercise 12–3   **Track: (CD 2, Track 23)**

		I	M	F
1.	full			
2.	oops			
3.	wolf			
4.	mutt			
5.	soot			
6.	goof			
7.	whoops			
8.	sugar			
9.	footstool			
10.	hood			

Transcription Exercise 12–4
Vowel: /ʊ/

 Track: (CD 2, Track 24)
Refer to Study Card: 36

Phonetic Symbol	Target Word	Transcription
/ʊ/	1. cook	
	2. wool	
	3. foot	
	4. wood	
	5. look	
	6. wolf	
	7. full	
	8. could	
	9. nook	

/ʊ/

Distinctive Features	Tongue Position
High back lax rounded vowel	Sides of back of tongue close lightly against upper molars; raised high in oral cavity.
	Tongue tip touches behind lower front teeth.
	Teeth are slightly open.
	Lips are rounded.
	Airflow is through the oral cavity.

Voicing/Velopharyngeal Port	Spelling Variations
Voiced—vocal folds *ad*duct.	oo b*oo*k, l*oo*k, w*oo*l
VP port is closed.	ou c*ou*ld, w*ou*ld

Word Position	Clinical Information
Medial position only in SAE	Also known as the upsilon or capped "u"

/o/

Transcription Exercise 12–5   **Track: (CD 2, Track 25)**

		I	M	F
1.	old			
2.	moot			
3.	sew			
4.	lotion			
5.	mow			
6.	who			
7.	cola			
8.	toast			
9.	bowl			
10.	macho			

Transcription Exercise 12–6
Vowel: /o/

 Track: (CD 2, Track 26)
Refer to Study Card: 37

Phonetic Symbol	Target Word	Transcription
/o/	1. note	
	2. tone	
	3. own	
	4. tote	
	5. know	
	6. oat	
	7. hone	
	8. no	
	9. owe	

/o/

Distinctive Features	Tongue Position
Mid-back tense rounded vowel	Body of tongue shifts slightly back of center and is raised.
	Tongue tip contacts lower front teeth.
	Lips round and protrude.

/O/

Voicing/Velopharyngeal Port	Spelling Variations
Voiced—vocal folds *ad*duct.	o *old,* g*o,* n*o*
VP port is closed.	oa c*oa*t, b*oa*t
	ow cr*ow,* kn*ow*
	oe d*oe*
	ew s*ew*

Word Positions	Clinical Information
Initial, medial, and final position in SAE	Some phoneticians refer to this phoneme as the diphthong /oʊ/

/ɔ/

Transcription Exercise 12–7   Track: (CD 2, Track 27)

		I	M	F
1.	all			
2.	thong			
3.	sauce			
4.	awe			
5.	schwa			
6.	moth			
7.	pa			
8.	squaw			
9.	paw			
10.	thought			

Transcription Exercise 12–8
Vowel: /ɔ/

 Track: (CD 2, Track 28)
Refer to Study Card: 38

Phonetic Symbol	Target Word	Transcription
/ɔ/	1. sought	
	2. bawdy	
	3. wrought	
	4. prawn	
	5. call	
	6. broad	
	7. thought	
	8. vault	
	9. unlawful	

Note: Dependent upon geographical location, speakers may use /ɑ/ when pronouncing these words.

/ɔ/

Distinctive Features	Tongue Position
Low Mid-back lax rounded vowel	Back and middle portion of tongue slightly raised; little and inconsistent contact with upper molars.
	Lips round and protrude.
/ɔ/	Airflow is through the oral cavity.

Voicing/Velopharyngeal Port	Spelling Variations
Voiced—vocal folds *ad*duct.	au *au*to, appl*au*se, l*au*ndry
VP port is closed.	aw *aw*e, l*aw*n, j*aw*
	augh(t) c*augh*t, t*augh*t
	o *o*ff, str*o*ng
	a b*a*ll, c*a*ll

Word Positions	Clinical Information
Initial, medial, and final position in SAE	Also referred to as the "open o" or "reversed c"

/a/

Transcription Exercise 12–9   Track: (CD 2, Track 29)

		I	M	F
1.	pasta			
2.	almond			
3.	spa			
4.	launch			
5.	genre			
6.	yacht			
7.	aqua			
8.	lunch			
9.	schwa			
10.	entree			

Transcription Exercise 12–10
Vowel: /ɑ/

 Track: (CD 2, Track 30)
Refer to Study Card: 39

Phonetic Symbol	Target Word	Transcription
/ɑ/	1. ah	
	2. not	
	3. ha	
	4. yacht	
	5. tot	
	6. yon	
	7. haunt	
	8. taught	
	9. aunt	

Note: Dependent upon geographical location, speakers may use /ɔ/ when pronouncing these words.

/ɑ/

Distinctive Features	Tongue Position
Low back lax unrounded vowel	Tongue is slightly raised in back.
	Tip touches behind lower front teeth.
	Lips do not round.

Voicing/Velopharyngeal Port	Spelling Variations
Voiced—vocal folds *add*uct.	o *pot, dot, olive*
VP port is closed.	a h*ear*t
	en *en*core

Word Positions	Clinical Information
Initial, medial, and final position in SAE	Used to transcribe the popular expression "ah"

Crossword Puzzle for /u/, /ʊ/, /o/, /ɑ/, and /ɔ/

Answers in Appendix B

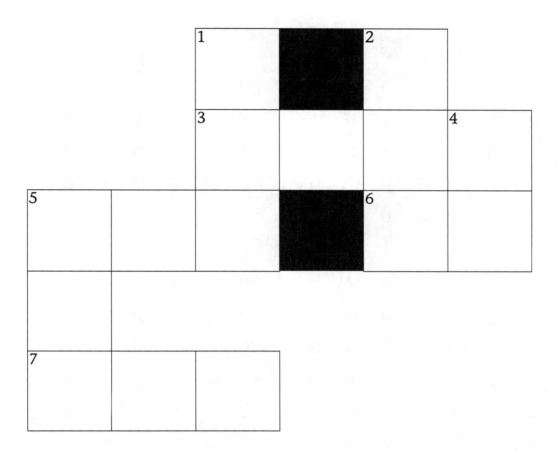

Directions: Transcribe the following words:

Across:
3. awful
5. long
6. toe
7. soak

Down:
1. thong
2. foot
4. low
5. loose

BACK VOWELS

Word Search #15   Answers in Appendix B

s ʃ r ɑ dʒ ɚ d ɔ l t r i z v m f ʍ
d ʒ ɚ k j u ə b ɑ ɑ z ð ʌ ʒ ɑ ɪ ɪ
b ʌ dʒ ɔ z j o r ɑ r i r ɛ v æ ʌ k
ʊ k p s θ i s ɑ ɛ t æ ɪ w m n u d
l r ɛ k h n dʒ b ʊ g s z ð e d o r
w ʌ p z s u z ɪ n l u tʃ i w p m ɔ
ɪ p v t ð i z n z ɪ l o p h ɑ d m
ŋ æ k s ʃ u ʍ h f n v ɛ o b k f ɑ
k s g t o θ p ʊ m p ʒ o p s ɛ ɪ g
l ɪ u æ l j h d ʊ g ŋ m n p t l r
b w f e w o k ʍ tʃ ɪ o u e i l z ɔ
h a i ə ʌ g ɑ r θ b r ʊ k s o g s
n k w tʃ æ z ʌ z h t w b v u n ʒ d
s ʍ ɪ k d r ɔ m ə g r ɔ j h i g t
j r u p ɔ l ɚ f ɛ ɚ b f dʒ u w e l
l ks ɪ dʒ o r dʒ b ʊ ʃ t s f z r s n

Directions: Find and circle the words which contain the /u/ʊ/o/ɑ/ɔ/ phonemes.

The Pope   Jewel

Garth Brooks   RuPaul

Ma and Pa Kettle   Robin Hood

George Bush   Quick Draw McGraw

Jaws   Susan Lucci

Transcription Exercise 12–11
Back Vowels: /u/ʊ/o/ɔ/ɑ/

 Track: (CD 2, Track 31)
Phoneme Study Cards: 35–39

1. coupon   _____

2. hook   _____

3. encore   _____

4. hawthorn   _____

5. newsroom   _____

6. taco   _____

7. yoyo   _____

8. awful   _____

9. yacht   _____

10. lollipop   _____

11. cookbook   _____

12. boastful   _____

13. footstool   _____

14. horseshoe   _____

15. fought   _____

16. dorm room   _____

17. fruit   _____

18. mothball   _____

19. soak   _____

20. thoughtful   _____

CHAPTER

13

Diphthongs

A *diphthong* represents two vowels that are spoken one after the other in continuation, as in saying a single vowel. The first vowel rapidly "glides" into the position of the second vowel. Simply, a diphthong begins by approximating the articulatory position of one vowel and ends by approximating the articulatory position of another vowel. It should be noted that *diphthong* can be pronounced in two ways: [dɪfθaŋ] or [dɪpθaŋ].

Diphthongs are not just the sum total of one vowel plus another but are a gradual movement of the articulators from one position to another. Figure 13–1 illustrates this movement. You will notice that the "capped a" is a component of the /aɪ/ and /aʊ/ diphthongs.

To indicate that the two vowel sounds in each diphthong are used together, a slur ‿ is used. The diphthongs /aɪ/ /aʊ/ and /ɔɪ/ are off-glides, made with the tongue moving from a lower vowel to a high vowel position. The /ju/ is an on-glide, with movement from a higher sound to a lower vowel position.

DIPHTHONGS

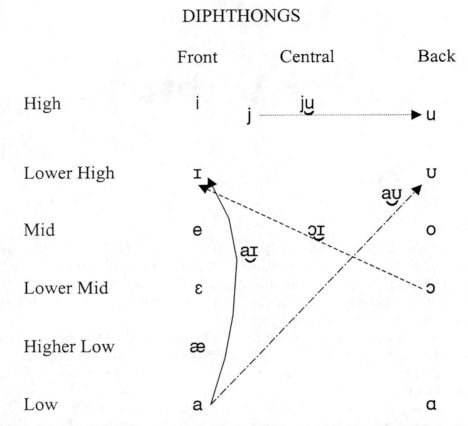

Figure 13–1. Movement of articulators when producing diphthongs.

/aɪ/

Transcription Exercise 13–1   Track: (CD 2, Track 32)

		I	M	F
1.	island			
2.	eye			
3.	guy			
4.	minus			
5.	dial			
6.	rhyme			
7.	sweet			
8.	high			
9.	niece			
10.	bride			

Transcription Exercise 13–2
Diphthong: /aɪ/

 Track: (CD 2, Track 33)
Refer to Study Card: 40

Phonetic Symbol	Target Word	Transcription
/aɪ/	1. buy	
	2. cider	
	3. height	
	4. feisty	
	5. slice	
	6. thyme	
	7. write	
	8. sigh	
	9. rhyme	

/aɪ/

Distinctive Features	Tongue Position
Rising low front to high front (off-glide) diphthong	Tongue is low in the oral cavity.
	Tongue moves from low front position of /a/ to high front position of /ɪ/.

/ɪ/

/a/

Voicing/Velopharyngeal Port	Spelling Variations
Voiced—vocal folds *ad*duct.	i w*i*ld, ch*i*ld, *i*dea
VP port is closed.	i-e b*i*ke, *i*ce, k*i*te
	y fr*y*, m*y*, wh*y*
	ie cr*ie*d, p*ie*, l*ie*
	igh - he*igh*t, n*igh*

Word Positions	Clinical Information
Initial, medial, and final positions in SAE	Also referred to as the "long i"

/aʊ/

Transcription Exercise 13–3   Track: (CD 2, Track 34)

		I	M	F
1.	ouch			
2.	lawn			
3.	coward			
4.	vowel			
5.	how			
6.	toffee			
7.	shout			
8.	know			
9.	lounge			
10.	house			

Transcription Exercise 13–4
Diphthong: /aʊ/

 Track: (CD 2, Track 35)
Refer to Study Card: 41

Phonetic Symbol	Target Word	Transcription
/aʊ/	1. oust	
	2. trout	
	3. gouging	
	4. prowl	
	5. chowder	
	6. household	
	7. bound	
	8. louse	
	9. bough	

/aʊ/

Distinctive Features	Tongue Position
Rising low front to high back (off-glide) diphthong	Tongue is in low front position for /a/ and glides back to high back position of /ʊ/.

Voicing/Velopharyngeal Port	Spelling Variations
Voiced—vocal folds *add*uct. VP port is closed.	ou *out*, h*ou*se, th*ou* ow *owl*, t*ow*n, v*ow*

Word Positions	Clinical Information
Initial, medial, and final positions in SAE	

/ɔɪ/

Transcription Exercise 13–5   **Track: (CD 2, Track 36)**

		I	M	F
1.	coy			
2.	choice			
3.	town			
4.	join			
5.	cipher			
6.	moist			
7.	mist			
8.	buoyant			
9.	juice			
10.	spoil			

Transcription Exercise 13–6
Diphthong: /ɔɪ/

 Track: (CD 2, Track 37)
Refer to Study Card: 42

Phonetic Symbol	Target Word	Transcription
/ɔɪ/	1. hoisting	
	2. coiled	
	3. destroy	
	4. foils	
	5. loiter	
	6. voicing	
	7. toy	
	8. exploit	
	9. avoid	

/ɔɪ/

Distinctive Features	Tongue Position
Rising mid-back to high front (off-glide) diphthong	Tongue glides from lower mid-back position of /ɔ/ to high front /ɪ/; lips unround.

/ɪ/

/ɔ/

Voicing/Velopharyngeal Port	Spelling Variations
Voiced—vocal folds *ad*duct. VP port is closed.	oi *oi*l, c*oi*n oy *oy*ster, l*oy*al, j*oy*

Word Position	Clinical Information
Initial, medial, and final positions in SAE	Also transcribed as /ɔɪ/

/ju/

Transcription Exercise 13–7 **Track: (CD 2, Track 38)**

		I	M	F
1.	few			
2.	union			
3.	beauty			
4.	cute			
5.	pew			
6.	use			
7.	huge			
8.	fool			
9.	humor			
10.	hula			

Transcription Exercise 13–8
Diphthong: /ju/

 Track: (CD 2, Track 39)
Refer to Study Card: 43

Phonetic Symbol	Target Word	Transcription
/ju/	1. ewe	
	2. fuchsia	
	3. music	
	4. huge	
	5. mutant	
	6. pupil	
	7. spewed	
	8. butte	
	9. fume	

/ju/

Distinctive Features	Tongue Position
High front to high back on-glide diphthong	Tip is at lower front teeth. Body of tongue is raised toward hard palate. Tongue moves to high back position of /u/.

Voicing/Velopharyngeal Port	Spelling Variations
Voiced—vocal folds *ad*duct. VP port is closed.	u *unit* u-e *use* eau b*eau*ty ew f*ew*

Word Positions	Clinical Information
Initial, medial, and final positions in SAE	

Crossword Puzzle for /aɪ/, /aʊ/, /ɔɪ/, and /ju/

Answers in Appendix B

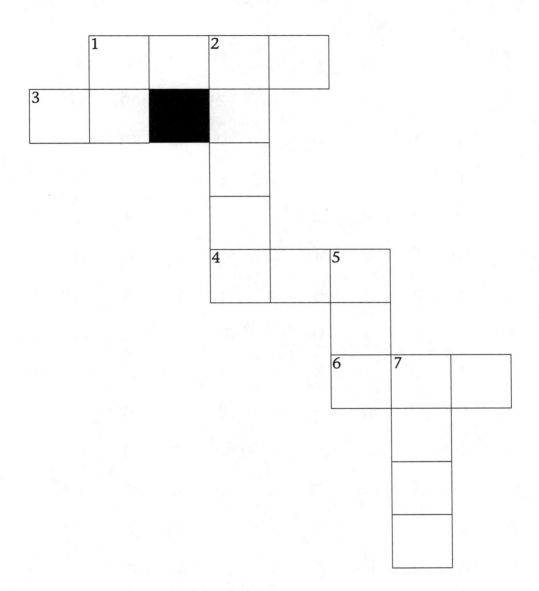

Across:
1. moist
3. cue
4. down
6. nine

Down:
1. mew
2. spoiled
5. noun
7. eyesight

DIPHTHONG

Word Search #16   Answers in Appendix B

```
s  ʃ  r  d  o  n  p  ɚ  r  ɔ  t  t  v
h  aɪ æ  k  s  v  ju z  p  n  ə  v  ʌ
d  s  t  ə  ɜ  ɔ  ɛ  b  ɔ  ɔɪ n  r  d
b  h  i  n  b  w  w  r  b  s  z  f  k
s  aʊ ɛ  t  k  z  ʌ  u  ʊ  t  i  h  p
h  s  aʊ θ  b  aʊ n  d  m  ɚ  b  ju s
f  p  ʒ  m  ɪ  g  z  i  m  ʒ  u  m  n
k  æ  w  aɪ l  d  f  aʊ l  æ  ʊ  ɚ  p
l  ɛ  t  n  æ  k  h  ʌ  ɪ  k  s  n  æ
b  b  s  θ  p  ə  r  z  d  p  i  g  s
h  ɪ  f  ŋ  s  ɔɪ l  v  z  ɔɪ v  ʒ  z
n  ju æ  l  ks dʒ t  ʃ  e  z  i  z  f
s  b  z  f  ju ʃ  ə  t  r  w  g  ɔ  aɪ
o  ɪ  k  aʊ tʃ g  j  r  æ  m  ɑ  ɚ  j
```

Directions: Find and circle the words listed below which contain the /aɪ/aʊ/ɔɪ/ju/ phonemes.

icehouse	wildfowl	soil
fuchsia	high	mine
poise	humor	oyster
you	views	couch
southbound		

Transcription Exercise 13–9
Diphthongs: /aɪ/aʊ/ɔɪ/ju/

 Track: (CD 2, Track 40)
Phoneme Study Cards: 40–43

1. foundry _____

2. join _____

3. Yukon _____

4. brine _____

5. toil _____

6. January _____

7. oust _____

8. ukulele _____

9. moist _____

10. amulet _____

11. pout _____

12. byte _____

13. noun _____

14. noise _____

15. frowning _____

16. I _____

17. contributor _____

18. oink _____

19. mime _____

20. brownies _____

CHAPTER

14

Word Stress

This chapter reviews the basics of stress. The term *stress* sometimes is used interchangeably with the term *accent*. Stress refers to the most prominent part of a syllable in a multisyllabic word or word within a phrase. More than the usual breath force creates this emphasis. Stressing syllables has been found to be associated with (a) high amplitude (loudness), (b) long duration of the syllable nucleus (time), and (c) high frequency (pitch) of the syllable nucleus.

In multisyllabic words, one syllable will receive more stress than the other. This is defined as word stress or lexical stress (Calvert, 1986). Determining stress is not always easy. American English speakers are familiar with word pronunciation. This is an area where English second-language learners can have difficulty. One way in which to determine what syllable is stressed in a multisyllabic word is to place the primary stress on the *wrong* syllable. In this way, the word will sound unusual.

Placement of Stress Marks

The International Phonetic Association alphabet suggests using three distinct stress levels in English multisyllabic words described as (a) *primary stress* ['], (b) *secondary stress* [,], and (c) no symbol to indicate *unstress*. A primary vertical line ['] is placed in *front* and *above* the syllable and a secondary vertical line [,] is placed *below* and in *front* of the syllable that receives secondary stress.

Here are some helpful hints to determine stress:

1 One-syllable words spoken in isolation always receive primary stress.

2 The majority of two-syllable words have stress on the first syllable.

3 Compound verbs have primary stress on the second verb, such as in "over*throw*."

4 Compound nouns have primary stress on the first syllable as in "*cup*cake."

The following words have primary stress on the *first* syllable:

*preach*er	*doll*ar
*use*ful	*cong*ress
*pill*ow	*reas*on

Contrast these words with the following words that have *second* syllable stress:

en*joy*   com*plete*

cas*cade*   im*mense*

ma*ture*   re*solve*

Reference

Calvert, D. (1986). *Descriptive phonetics.* New York: Thieme Medical Publishers.

CHAPTER

15

Dynamics of Connected Speech

Introduction

By the time you read this chapter, you have spent numerous hours studying the IPA to memorize the phonetic symbols and completing the Transcription Exercises. In this chapter, you will learn about the interesting changes in words that can occur during speech. The renowned linguist, Peter Ladefoged, compares the rapid tongue movements required for speech to that of a concert pianist's rapid finger movements (2005, p. 185). During speech, considerable effort is expended by muscles of the tongue, jaw, lips, velum, and laryngeal region to produce the finely timed precision movements required to distinctly articulate each phoneme. According to Shipley and McAfee (1998), conversational speech is uttered at the incredible speed of 270 words per minute.

To cope with this task of articulating extremely rapid changes from phoneme to phoneme, *accommodation* occurs. Accommodation is an adjustment or adaptation of a speech sound as a result of the *phonetic environment* (or *context*) of a phoneme. Phonetic environment describes the phonemes that surround a specific speech sound. There are two types of accommodation, *assimilation* and *coarticulation*.

Assimilation produces major changes that occur when a phoneme is omitted, added, or changed to a different phoneme.

Coarticulation produces minor changes in phonemes. Phoneticians disagree on whether the processes of coarticulation and assimilation are two distinct processes or are similar. We support McKay (1987) in his view of two processes.

Assimilation

There are two types of assimilation: *progressive* and *regressive assimilation*. These types of assimilation can result in a change in place of production and/or voicing of a phoneme.

Progressive Assimilation

Say the word "dogs." When articulated, the word is transcribed as [dɑgz]. Progressive assimilation has occurred in this word in a left to right pattern. The voicing of the /g/ has influenced the unvoiced /s/, changing it into the voiced /z/. The *preceding* phoneme /g/ has influenced the phoneme which follows, /s/. Progressive assimilation occurs as a function of *morphology*, or the study of *morphemes*. According to McLaughlin (2006), a *morpheme* is a minimal, meaningful unit of language. Of the two types of morphemes, free and bound, we will focus on the *bound* morphemes, which must be attached to a word.

Some examples of these are the -s [kafs] and -z forms [sʌnz] and the past tense -t [rekt]. Transcription Exercise 15–1 will give you practice for this concept.

Another example of progressive assimilation occurs in the word "horseshoe." The final sound of /s/ in "horse" is completely assimilated into the prolonged initial sound of "shoe" /ʃ/, so the word is transcribed as [horʃʃu].

Regressive Assimilation

In contrast to progressive assimilation, the effects of regressive assimilation occur in a right to left manner. In this type of assimilation, a phoneme is changed by the phoneme that *follows* it. For example, in the word "bank," the /k/ influences the preceding /n/ phoneme by changing it into an /ŋ/. The correct transcription would be [beŋk].

Unless each phoneme is produced with a pause before and after as in "b-a-n-k" (which would sound unusual), the effects of regressive assimilation cannot be avoided. The reason this occurs is that the place of articulation of the /k/ (lingua-velar) affects the place of articulation of the /n/ (lingua-alveolar), and the /n/ *assimilates* the place of articulation of the /ŋ/, which is also a lingua-velar.

Transcription Exercise 15–1 contains opportunities for transcription of words with regressive assimilation.

Phonemes can also be omitted during speech. The word "veteran" [vɛtə-ɪn] is often pronounced [vɛtrɪn]. Omission, also called *elision*, occurs very frequently in phrases. The phrase, "Where have you been?" can be shortened to [wɛrjʌbɪn].

In contrast to phoneme elimination, some sounds can be added, a process known as *epenthesis* or *intrusion*. The /t/ phoneme is a common intrusive sound, especially when a nasal sound is followed by an unvoiced sound. Say the word "mince." An interesting thing occurs when the word "mince" is articulated. Unless we pause between saying the /n/ and /s/ sounds (which would sound unusual), the word is articulated as [mɪnᵗs]. You will notice the addition of the /t/ which has been intruded. In producing the word "mince," the tongue is at the alveolar ridge for the /n/, which is also where the /s/ is produced. To make articulation easier, the tongue *remains* at the alveolar ridge, with the result of the intruded /t/. The /n,s,t/ are all produced in the same *place* of articulation. Intrusion is defined as the addition of a sound which is not included in the spelling of the word but which occurs when the word is articulated.

Remember that the intruded sound may or not be audible, but is present because it is articulated. Some phoneticians choose to raise the intruded /t/ when a word is transcribed. Intrusion is a result of the speed with which we speak and economical articulatory movements.

The /p/ and /k/ phonemes are also subject to intrusion. The word "warmth" is transcribed as [wormpθ] with the intrusion of the /p/. In order to eliminate the intruded /p/, the speaker would have to pause between saying the /m/ and the /θ/. An example of the intruded /k/ occurs in the word "length," which is articulated as [leŋkθ]. Try saying each phoneme separately in the word "length," and then say the word as you normally would by blending the sounds together.

Unlike the /t/p/k/, which intrude in the phonetic context of other consonants, the /j/ and /w/ can intrude between vowels. In the phrase "see it," the /j/ intrudes between the final position vowel of the first word /i/ and the initial vowel /ɪ/ of the word which follows, as in [sijɪt]. The phrase "two apples" provides an example of the intruded /w/, as in [tuwæpəlz]. If the words in the phrases were said separately, the intrusion of /j/ and /w/ would not occur.

Coarticulation

The other type of accommodation is coarticulation. Compared to the major changes in assimilation, coarticulation produces *minor* phonetic changes. Coarticulation occurs as a result of a fast rate of speech. Say the word "moon." Did you notice that your lips were already in position for the /u/ when you were producing the /m/? In Stan-dard American English, vowels are normally produced without nasal resonance except when they appear before or after a nasal consonant, as in [mæn]. This nasality is indicated by the /~/ symbol placed over the sound that has acquired nasal resonance. Symbols that indicate a specific way a pho-neme has been produced are termed *diacritics.* This is *narrow transcription,* which uses dia-critics to specifically explain how a sound was produced. Contrast this with *broad tran-scription* which uses only the IPA phoneme symbol to represent a sound.

Frequently used diacritics are listed in Table 15–1. S. Singh and K. Singh (2006) provide an expanded list of diacritics.

Often in conversational speech we extend the duration of a sound, known as *length-ening* or *prolongation.* This occurs frequently when we say two words together, one of which ends in the same sound as the begin-ning sound of the adjacent word. For exam-ple, the phrase "same milk" can be produced as [sem:ɪlk]. The lengthening diacritic [:] *fol-lows* the prolonged phoneme.

Table 15–1. Selected Diacritics

Diacritic	Name	Example	Affects	Phoneme(s)
[ʰ]	Aspirated	[pʰost]	Voiceless stops	/p/, /t/, /k/
[˺]	Unreleased	[bæk˺drɔp]	All plosives	/p/, /b/, /t/, /d/, /k/, /g/
[˜]	Nasality	[nõt]	Vowels adjacent to nasals	All vowels & diphthongs
[̥]	Unvoiced	[pr̥ɑɪ]	Follows voiceless consonants	/r/
[ˬ]	Voiced	[bɛt̬ɚ]	Adjacent to voiced sounds	/t/, /s/
[̩]	Syllabic consonant	[bʌtn̩] [æpl̩]	Lateral and nasals	/l/, /n/, /m/, /ŋ/
[:]	Prolongation	[dɑːrk]	Emphasized phonemes	Possible with any phonemes

We can say the phrase "both thumbs" as two separate words, or joined together as in [boθːʌmz]. The diacritic [ː] is used to indicate lengthening. Some examples are provided in Transcription Exercise 15–1.

Another change that can occur in speech is *devoicing*. Devoicing occurs when a voiced phoneme becomes unvoiced due to the phonetic environment, but the voiced phoneme does *not* become totally voiceless. The phonetic environment for devoicing is when a voiced phoneme follows an unvoiced phoneme, as in the word "pray" [pr̥e]. The devoicing diacritic is a small circle / ̥ / *under* the devoiced phoneme.

Here is a silly sentence that uses the diacritics discussed in this chapter:

Put these zany dogs in the backdoor of the clean critter kennel.

[pʊtʰ ðizːeñi dagz ɪn ði bæk˺ dor ʌv ði kl̥in kr̥ɪt̬ɚ kɛnl̩]

References

Ladefoged, P. (2005). *Vowels and consonants* (2nd ed.). Malden, MA: Blackwell.

MacKay, I. (1987). *Phonetics: The science of speech production.* Boston: Allyn and Bacon.

McLaughlin, S. (2006). *Introduction to language development* (2nd ed.). Clifton Park, NY: Thomson Delmar Learning.

Shipley, K., & McAfee, J. (1998). *Assessment in speech-language pathology. A resource manual* (2nd ed.). San Diego, CA: Singular.

Singh, S., & Singh, K. (2006). *Phonetics: Principles and practices* (3rd ed.). San Diego, CA: Plural.

Transcription Exercise 15–1   **Track: (CD 2, Track 41)**

These words contain examples of (1) progressive assimilation, (2) regressive assimilation, (3) intrusion, (4) lengthening, and (5) omission.

1. fixed (1)   _____

2. cancel (3)   _____

3. stop pushing (4)   _____

4. junk (2)   _____

5. pushed (1)   _____

6. dreamt (3)   _____

7. go away (5)   _____

8. wigs (1)   _____

9. mink (2)   _____

10. little Lucy (4)   _____

11. fragrance (2)   _____

12. stomachs (1)   _____

13. kiss her (5)   _____

14. comfort (3)   _____

15. black corn (4)   _____

16. bugs (1)   _____

17. let me go (5)   _____

18. prince (3)   _____

19. seeds (1)   _____

20. thin knife (4)   _____

CHAPTER

16

Dialect Differences

The focus of this Workbook is phoneme production in Standard American English (SAE). SAE is "accent-free." This is the type of speech you hear when you listen to national broadcasters present the news on television and radio. A *dialect* is a speech or language variation. We refer to an *accent* when we discuss speech that has characteristics of a foreign dialect.

There are several United States dialects representative of various geographical regions including the East, Midwest, and Southern states. Each region has specific variations in pronunciation and language. Refer to sources at the end of this chapter, which present a discussion of dialects.

Speakers of African American English use specific speech substitutions. These are presented in Table 16–1. Foreign accents in the Arabic, Hispanic, and Asian dialects are included in Tables 16–2, 16–3, and 16–4, respectively.

Goldstein (2000) offers a detailed discussion of linguistic diversity, as do Butler (1994) and Coleman (2000).

References

Butler, K. (1994). *Cross-cultural perspectives in language assessment and intervention.* Gaithersburg, MD: Aspen.

Coleman, T. J. (2000). *Clinical and linguistic diversity resource guide for speech-language pathologists.* San Diego, CA: Singular.

Goldstein, B. (2000). *Cultural and linguistic diversity resource guide for speech-language pathologists.* Boston: Allyn and Bacon.

Roseberry-McKibbin, C. (2002). *Multicultural students with special language needs: Practical strategies for assessment and intervention.* Oceanside, CA: Academic Communication Associates.

Table 16–1. Characteristics of African American English Articulation and Phonology

Articulation Characteristics	Sample English Utterances
/l/ phoneme lessened or omitted	too'/tool a'ways/always
/r/ phoneme lessened or omitted	doah/door mudah/mother p'otect/protect
f/voiceless "th" substitution at the end or middle of a word	teef/teeth bof/both nufin'/nothing
t/voiceless "th" substitution at the beginning of a word	tink/think tin/thin
d/voiced "th" substitution at the beginning or middle of a word	dis/this broder/brother
v/voiced "th" substitution at the end of a word	breave/breathe smoov/smooth
Consonant cluster reduction	des'/desk res'/rest lef'/left was'/wasp
Differing syllable stress patterns	gui tar/guitar po lice/police Ju ly/July

Table 16–2. Articulation and Language Differences Commonly Observed among Arabic Speakers

Articulation Characteristics	Sample English Utterances	
n/ng substitution	son/song	nothin'/nothing
sh/ch substitution	mush/much	shoe/chew
w/v or f/v substitution	west/vest fife/five	Walerie/Valerie abofe/above
t/voiceless "th" or s/voiceless "th" substitution	bat/bath sing/thing	noting/nothing somesing/something
z/voiced "th" substitution	brozer/brother	zese/these
zh/j substitution	zhoke/joke	fuzh/fudge
Retroflex /r/ does not exist	Speakers of Arabic will use a tap or trilled /r/.	
There are no triple consonant clusters in Arabic, so epenthesis may occur	kinduhly/kindly	harduhly/hardly
o/a substitutions	hole/hall	bowl/ball
o/oi substitutions	bowl/boil	foble/foible
uh/ae substitutions	snuck/snack	ruck/rack
i/ɪ substitutions	cheep/chip	sheep/ship
Language Characteristics	**Sample English Utterances**	
Omission of possessives 's and "of"	That Kathy book. The title the story is . . .	
Omission of plurals	She has 5 horse in her stable. He has 3 pen in his pocket.	
Omissions of prepositions	Put your shoes.	
Omission of the form "to be"	She _____ my friend	
Inversion of noun constructs	Let's go to the station gas.	

Source: From *Multicultural Students with Special Language Needs: Practical Strategies for Assessment and Intervention* (Table 9–2, p. 161), by C. Roseberry-McKibbin, 2002, Oceanside, CA: Academic Communication Associates. Copyright 2002 by Academic Communication Associates. Reprinted with permission.

Table 16–3. Articulation Differences Commonly Observed among Spanish Speakers

Articulation Characteristics	Sample English Utterances
/t, d, n/ may be dentalized (tip of tongue is placed against the back of the upper central incisors)	
Final consonants are often devoiced.	dose/doze
b/v substitution	berry/very
Deaspirated stops (sounds like the speaker is omitting the sound because it is said with little air released).	
ch/sh substitution	chew/shoe
Voiced and voiceless "th" do not exist in Spanish.	dis/this tink/think zat/that
Schwa sound is inserted before word initial consonant clusters.	eskate/skate espend/spend
Words end in vowels only or in just a few consonants (/l, r, n, s, d/).	Speakers may delete many final consonants in English.
When words start with an "h", the "h" is silent.	'old/hold, 'it/hit
/r/ is tapped or trilled (tap /r/ might sound like the tap in the English word "butter")	
"j" (e.g., judge) does not exist in Spanish; speakers may substitute the "y."	Yulie/Julie yoke/joke
The Spanish "s" is produced more frontally than the English "s."	Some speakers may sound like they have frontal lisps.
The ñ is produced as "ny" (e.g., baño is pronounced " bahnyo").	
Spanish has 5 vowels (ɑ,ɛ,i,o,u) and few diphthongs. Thus, Spanish speakers may produce the following vowel substitutions:	
i/ɪ substitution	peeg/pig leetle/little
ɛ/æ, ɑ/æ	pet/pat Stahn, Stan

Source: From *Multicultural Students with Special Language Needs: Practical Strategies for Assessment and Intervention* (Table 5–2, p. 85), by C. Roseberry-McKibbin, 2002, Oceanside, CA: Academic Communication Associates. Copyright 2002 by Academic Communication Associates. Reprinted with permission.

Table 16–4. Articulation Differences Commonly Observed among Asian Speakers

Articulation Characteristics	Sample English Utterances	
In many Asian languages, words end in vowels only or in just a few consonants; speakers may delete many final consonants in English	ste/step ro/robe	li/lid do/dog
Some languages are monosyllabic; speakers may truncate polysyllabic words or emphasize the wrong syllable	efunt/elephant **di**versity/diversity (emphasis on the first syllable)	
Possible devoicing of voiced cognates	beece/bees luff/love	pick/pig crip/crib
r/l confusion	lize/rize	clown/crown
/r/ may be omitted entirely	gull/girl	
Reduction of vowel length in words	Words sound choppy to Americans.	
No voiced or voiceless "th"	dose/those zose/those	tin/thin sin/thin
Epenthesis (addition of "uh" sound in blends or at the end of words)	bulack/black	wooduh/wood
Confusion of "ch" and "sh"	sheep/cheap	beesh/beach
/ae/ does not exist in many Asian languages	block/black	shock/shack
b/v substitutions	base/vase	Beberly/Beverly
v/w substitutions	vork/work	vall/wall

Source: From *Multicultural Students with Special Language Needs: Practical Strategies for Assessment and Intervention* (Table 6–3, p. 109), by C. Roseberry-McKibbin, 2002, Oceanside, CA: Academic Communication Associates. Copyright 2002 by Academic Communication Associates. Reprinted with permission.

International Phonetic Alphabet

CONSONANTS (PULMONIC)

	Bilabial	Labiodental	Dental	Alveolar	Postalveolar	Retroflex	Palatal	Velar	Uvular	Pharyngeal	Glottal
Plosive	p b			t d		ʈ ɖ	c ɟ	k ɡ	q ɢ		ʔ
Nasal	m	ɱ		n		ɳ	ɲ	ŋ	ɴ		
Trill	ʙ			r					ʀ		
Tap or Flap				ɾ		ɽ					
Fricative	ɸ β	f v	θ ð	s z	ʃ ʒ	ʂ ʐ	ç ʝ	x ɣ	χ ʁ	ħ ʕ	h ɦ
Lateral fricative				ɬ ɮ							
Approximant		ʋ		ɹ		ɻ	j	ɰ			
Lateral approximant				l		ɭ	ʎ	ʟ			

Where symbols appear in pairs, the one to the right represents a voiced consonant. Shaded areas denote articulations judged impossible.

CONSONANTS (NON-PULMONIC)

Clicks		Voiced implosives		Ejectives	
ʘ	Bilabial	ɓ	Bilabial	ʼ	Examples:
ǀ	Dental	ɗ	Dental/alveolar	pʼ	Bilabial
ǃ	(Post)alveolar	ʄ	Palatal	tʼ	Dental/alveolar
ǂ	Palatoalveolar	ɠ	Velar	kʼ	Velar
ǁ	Alveolar lateral	ʛ	Uvular	sʼ	Alveolar fricative

VOWELS

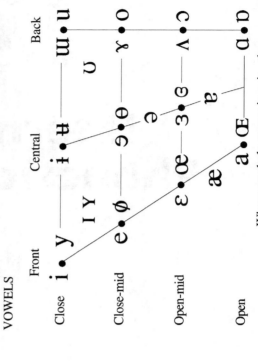

Where symbols appear in pairs, the one to the right represents a rounded vowel.

OTHER SYMBOLS

ʍ Voiceless labial-velar fricative

w Voiced labial-velar approximant

ɥ Voiced labial-palatal approximant

ʜ Voiceless epiglottal fricative

ʢ Voiced epiglottal fricative

ʡ Epiglottal plosive

ɕ ʑ Alveolo-palatal fricatives

ɺ Alveolar lateral flap

ɧ Simultaneous ʃ and x

Affricates and double articulations can be represented by two symbols joined by a tie bar if necessary.

k͡p t͡s

SUPRASEGMENTALS

ˈ Primary stress

ˌ Secondary stress ˌfoʊnəˈtɪʃən

ː Long eː

ˑ Half-long eˑ

˘ Extra-short ĕ

| Minor (foot) group

‖ Major (intonation) group

. Syllable break ɹi.ækt

‿ Linking (absence of a break)

TONES AND WORD ACCENTS

LEVEL			CONTOUR	
e̋ or ˥	Extra high	ě or ˩˥	Rising	
é ˦	High	ê ˥˩	Falling	
ē ˧	Mid	e᷄ ˧˥	High rising	
è ˨	Low	e᷅ ˩˧	Low rising	
ȅ ˩	Extra low	e᷈ ˧˩˧	Rising-falling	
ꜜ →	Downstep	↗	Global rise	
ꜛ ←	Upstep	↘	Global fall	

DIACRITICS Diacritics may be placed above a symbol with a descender, e.g. ŋ̊

Voiceless	̥	n̥ d̥	Breathy voiced	̤	b̤ a̤	Dental	̪	t̪ d̪
Voiced	̬	s̬ t̬	Creaky voiced	̰	b̰ a̰	Apical	̺	t̺ d̺
Aspirated	ʰ	tʰ dʰ	Linguolabial	̼	t̼ d̼	Laminal	̻	t̻ d̻
More rounded	̹	ɔ̹	Labialized	ʷ	tʷ dʷ	Nasalized	̃	ẽ
Less rounded	̜	ɔ̜	Palatalized	ʲ	tʲ dʲ	Nasal release	ⁿ	dⁿ
Advanced	̟	u̟	Velarized	ˠ	tˠ dˠ	Lateral release	ˡ	dˡ
Retracted	̠	e̠	Pharyngealized	ˤ	tˤ dˤ	No audible release	̚	d̚
Centralized	̈	ë	Velarized or pharyngealized	̴	ɫ			
Mid-centralized	̽	e̽	Raised	̝	e̝ (ɹ̝ = voiced alveolar fricative)			
Syllabic	̩	n̩	Lowered	̞	e̞ (β̞ = voiced bilabial approximant)			
Non-syllabic	̯	e̯	Advanced Tongue Root	̘	e̘			
Rhoticity	˞	ɚ a˞	Retracted Tongue Root	̙	e̙			

Answers to Exercises

Chapter 2

Transcription Exercise 2–1
Track: (CD 1, Track 2)

Number of Sounds			Transcription
2	1.	gnaw	[nɔ]
3	2.	shape	[ʃep]
5	3.	cousin	[kʌzɪn]
4	4.	leisure	[liʒɚ]
3	5.	tongue	[tʌŋ]
2	6.	who	[hu]
4	7.	rather	[ræðɚ]
3	8.	tough	[tʌf]
3	9.	kneel	[nil]
3	10.	ax	[æks]
7	11.	cinnamon	[sɪnʌmɪn]
3	12.	wrap	[ræp]
4	13.	raked	[rekt]
3	14.	sight	[saɪt]
5	15.	phoneme	[fonim]

Transcription Exercise 2–2
Track: (CD 1, Track 3)

[præktɪs ɛvɚi de]

Transcription Exercise 2–3
Track: (CD 1, Track 4)

Consonants	Vowels
1. /k/	7. /u/
2. /ŋ/	8. /i/
3. /dʒ/	9. /o/
4. /f/	10. /ɝ/
5. /j/	11. /e/
6. /z/	12. /ɑ/

Chapter 4

Transcription Exercise 4–1

1. [fon]
2. [splɪt]   M
3. [hɪkəp]   F
4. [gofɚ]
5. [ʃapɪŋ]   M
6. [prɛsɪdɛnt] I
7. [pɛpɚmɪnt] I & M
8. [numætɪk]
9. [əpɛnd]   M
10. [pæmflɪt]   I

/p/ Transcription Exercise 4–2
Track: (CD 1, Track 6)

1. [paɪn]
2. [dip]
3. [əˈpoz]
4. [kep]
5. [ˈpepɚ]
6. [sɪp]
7. [ples]
8. [hɛlp]
9. [pæk]

/b/ Transcription Exercise 4–3
Track: (CD 1, Track 7)

1. [hʌmbəl]   M
2. [rɪbɪn]   M
3. [bilebɚ]   I & M
4. [pʌblɪk]   M
5. [bɝbæŋk]   I & M
6. [θʌm]
7. [prob]   F
8. [hælɪbʌt]   M
9. [brok]   I
10. [tumston]

/b/ Transcription Exercise 4–4
Track: (CD 1, Track 8)

1. [bæd]
2. [tʌb]
3. [ˈbebi]
4. [braɪt]
5. [ˈræbɪt]
6. [ˈnobədi]
7. [bɔm]
8. [kɔb]
9. [kɝb]

/p/ and /b/ Crossword

Across	Down
1. [paliwag]	1. [pɛbəl]
3. [kʌb]	2. [lipɪŋ]
4. [pʌmps]	
5. [brɪŋ]	

/t/ Transcription Exercise 4–5
Track: (CD 1, Track 9)

1. [kɔt]   F
2. [wɪsəl]
3. [tuwɪʃɪn]   I
4. [taɪm]   I

5. [tɛntətɪv]   I & M
6. [tortijə]   I & M
7. [watʃt]   F
8. [ʃæle]
9. [tɛɪtori]   I & M
10. [moʃən]

t/ Transcription Exercise 4–6
Track: (CD 1, Track 10)

1. [tʌb]
2. [kʌt]
3. ['ɪntu]
4. ['ʌntɪl]
5. [twɪn]
6. [kot]
7. ['rotet]
8. [tɑɪm]
9. [nɛst]

Glottal Stop Transcription Exercise 4–7
Track: (CD 1, Track 11)

1. ['dulɪtəl]   [dulɪʔl̩]
2. ['mɪtən]   [mɪʔn̩]
3. ['faʊntən]   [faʊnʔn̩]
4. ['pætənt]   [pæʔnt]
5. ['hɪltən]   [hɪlʔn̩]
6. ['bʌtən]   [bʌʔn̩]
7. ['lætən]   [læʔn̩]
8. ['kɔtən]   [kɔʔn̩]
9. ['bɪtən]   [bɪʔn̩]
10. ['moltən]   [molʔn̩]

Voiced /t/ Transcription Exercise 4–8
Track: (CD 1, Track 12)

1. ['bɛtɚ]   ['bɛt̬ɚ]
2. ['hɔtɚ]   ['hɔt̬ɚ]
3. ['bætəl]   ['bæt̬əl]
4. ['mætɚ]   ['mæt̬ɚ]
5. ['ætəm]   ['æt̬əm]
6. ['bʌtɚ]   ['bʌt̬ɚ]
7. ['ketɚ]   ['ket̬ɚ]
8. ['kwotə]   ['kwot̬ə]
9. ['tʃɪtɪd]   ['tʃɪt̬ɪd]
10. ['duti]   ['dut̬i]

/d/ Transcription Exercise 4–9
Track: (CD 1, Track 13)

1. [hɛdʒ]
2. [hæŋkɚtʃɪf]
3. [mæpt]

4. [dɛdɪnd]   I & M & F
5. [dɛked]   I & F
6. [pɔɪntɛd]   F
7. [ædɪŋ]   M
8. [midijəl]   M
9. [drɛd]   I & F
10. [dimænd]   I & F

/d/ Transcription Exercise 4–10
Track: (CD 1, Track 14)

1. [do]
2. ['kʌndɪʃən]
3. [juzd]
4. [dɪʃ]
5. ['mɛdo]
6. [sænd]
7. [dwɛl]
8. ['wʌndɚ]
9. ['tʃendʒd]

/t/ and /d/ Crossword Puzzle

Across	Down
1. [dɛf]	1. [dɑɪmz]
2. [dɪziz]	2. [dituɚ]
3. [detə]	3. [dɑt]

/k/ Transcription Exercise 4–11
Track: (CD 1, Track 15)

1. [sɛntɪmitɚ]
2. [pike]   M
3. [kwortet]   I
4. [tɛkst]   M
5. [brɑŋkɑɪtɪs] M
6. [ɪmpɛkəbəl] M
7. [krɪtɪk]   I & F
8. [bækek]   M & F
9. [nɑɪt]
10. [tokvɪl]   M

/k/ Transcription Exercise 4–12
Track: (CD 1, Track 16)

1. [bæk]
2. [kaʊnt]
3. [tɪk]
4. ['bæskɪt]
5. [kek]
6. [krim]
7. ['stakɪŋ]
8. [ə'kras]
9. [mɑr'ki]

/g/ Transcription Exercise 4–13
Track: (CD 1, Track 17)

1. [dʒɛntəl]
2. [garbɪdʒ]   I
3. [næt]
4. [ɛgnag]   M & F
5. [ɛgzɪst]   M
6. [gaʊdʒ]   I
7. [læf]
8. [gɝtrud]   I
9. [lɪŋgɚ]   M
10. [dɪdʒɪt]

/g/ Transcription Exercise 4–14
Track: (CD 1, Track 18)

1. [gan]
2. ['wɪgəl]
3. ['hʌŋgri]
4. [bɛg]
5. [dɔg]
6. [grin]
7. [veg]
8. [glʌv]
9. ['grɪdəl]

/k/ and /g/ Crossword Puzzle

Across	Down
2. [ʃʊgɚ]	1. [jogɚt]
3. [brɛkfɛst]	3. [bekən]
5. [kɔfi]	4. [ɛgz]
6. [næpkɪn]	

Stop-Consonant Transcription Exercise 4–15
Track: (CD 1, Track 19)

1. ['pɝpɪtret]   11. ['pʌgodə]
2. ['bʌkɪt]   12. ['bɝdbik]
3. ['klepat]   13. [fɪkst]
4. [drapt]   14. ['læptap]
5. [pop]   15. ['gæbi]
6. [datudat]   16. ['dagtæg]
7. ['kʌpkek]   17. ['bækʌp]
8. ['bebid]   18. ['togə]
9. ['dɛdbolt]   19. [pɔkɪtbʊk]
10. [kot]   20. [kɛpt]

Chapter 5

/m/ Transcription Exercise 5–1
Track: (CD 1, Track 20)

1. [mɝmed]   I & M
2. [daɪm]   F
3. [pam]   F
4. [mʌm]   I & F
5. [kæzəm]   F
6. [mɪnɪmʌm]   I & M & F
7. [mɛmbren]   I & M
8. [hæmɚ]   M
9. [skwɝm]   F
10. [ɛmpaɪjɚ]   M

/m/ Transcription Exercise 5–2
Track: (CD 1, Track 21)

1. [maɪt]
2. [læmp]
3. [mit]
4. [tim]
5. ['kæmɚə]
6. [malt]
7. ['rændəm]
8. [harm]
9. [smɛl]

/n/ Transcription Exercise 5–3
Track: (CD 1, Track 22)

1. [næpsæk]   I
2. [kɪnəl]   M
3. [nansɛnᵗs]   I & M
4. [zon]   F
5. [prɛŋk]
6. [numætɪk]   I
7. [nun]   I & F
8. [nom]   I
9. [bigɪnɚ]   M
10. [sɛvɪntin]   F

/n/ Transcription Exercise 5–4
Track: (CD 1, Track 23)

1. ['tɛnɪs]
2. ['kæbɪn]
3. ['nɔɪzi]
4. ['kʌnɛri]
5. ['nɔtɪkəl]
6. ['vaɪolɪn]
7. ['hændi]
8. ['pænəl]
9. ['naɪlɔn]

/ŋ/ Transcription Exercise 5–5
Track: (CD 1, Track 24)

1. [mʌŋki]   M
2. [sɪŋɪŋ]   M & F
3. [kɪŋdʌm]   M
4. [ʌrendʒ]
5. [ilaŋget]   M
6. [rɔŋ]   F
7. [dʒɪŋgəl]   M
8. [leŋkθ]   M
9. [feŋz]   M
10. [spʌndʒ]

/ŋ/ Transcription Exercise 5–6
Track: (CD 1, Track 25)

1. ['bɔŋgo]
2. ['straŋgli]
3. ['haŋkaŋ]
4. [wɪŋ]
5. [tʌŋ]
6. ['ʃɪŋgəl]
7. ['daɪnɪŋ]
8. [feŋ]
9. ['sevɪŋz]

/m/ /n/ and /ŋ/ Crossword Puzzle

Across
1. [naɪn]
3. [kɪŋdəm]
4. [numonjə]

Down
1. [næpkɪn]
2. [stim]

Nasal Consonant Transcription Exercise 5–7
Track: (CD 1, Track 26)

1. ['nezəl]
2. ['manjʊmɛntəl]
3. [ə'mʌŋ]
4. [remnɪnt]
5. [nɔmɪnet]
6. [fɛmɪnɪn]
7. [lɛmoned]
8. ['mornɪŋ]
9. ['tʃɪmni]
10. ['mitɪŋ]
11. ['kʌntenɪŋ]
12. ['mɪŋglɪŋ]
13. [mɛmbren]
14. ['mʌni]
15. ['næni]
16. ['mɝ-eŋ]
17. ['maʊntɪn]
18. [numɛrɪkəl]
19. [sɪnə'mʌn]
20. ['munbim]

Chapter 6
/f/ Transcription Exercise 6–1
Track: (CD 1, Track 27)

1. [fasforəs]   I & M
2. [pæmflɪt]   M

3. [dʒɝ-æf]   F
4. [foto]   I
5. [fɪftin]   I & M
6. [dʒosɪf]   F
7. [sfɪrɪkəl]   M
8. [manogræf]   F
9. [flʌfi]   I & M
10. [fonəgræf]   I & F

/f/ Transcription Exercise 6–2
Track: (CD 1, Track 28)

1. [fʌn]
2. [bi'for]
3. ['fɪftin]
4. [frast]
5. ['kɔfi]
6. [lif]
7. [læf]
8. [flot]
9. [ɪf]

/v/ Transcription Exercise 6–3
Track: (CD 1, Track 29)

1. [vɪndɪktɪv]   I & F
2. [waɪf]
3. [ʃevran]   M
4. [wivɚ]   F
5. [ʌv]   F
6. [laɪfsevɪŋ]   M
7. [nɛvɚ]   M
8. [waɪvz]   M
9. [vɛrɪfaɪ]   I
10. [stov]   F

/v/ Transcription Exercise 6–4
Track: (CD 1, Track 30)

1. [vaɪn]
2. ['vɛlvɪt]
3. ['ovɚ]
4. ['veri]
5. ['ɪnvaɪt]
6. [lɪv]
7. ['væljʊ]
8. [wivɚ]
9. [muv]

/f/ and /v/ Crossword Puzzle

Across
1. [kæfin]
4. [ves]
5. [flɪp]

Down
1. [kævɪti]
2. [fɛstɪvəl]
3. [notɪfaɪ]

/s/ Transcription Exercise 6–5
Track: (CD 1, Track 31)

1. [sɪti]   I
2. [ʃevz]
3. [dɪsɛptɪv]   M
4. [blɪnts]   F
5. [juʒjul]
6. [æksɪz]   M
7. [breslɪt]   M
8. [aɪlɪnd]
9. [sudo]   I
10. [braŋks]   F

/s/ Transcription Exercise 6–6
Track: (CD 1, Track 32)

1. [ɛls]
2. [ə'slɪp]
3. [su'pirijɚ]
4. ['besɪn]
5. ['istɚ]
6. ['sidɚ]
7. [æsks]
8. ['sændəl]
9. [blæst]

/z/ Transcription Exercise 6–7
Track: (CD 1, Track 33)

1. [kɪdz]   F
2. [zar]   I
3. [tʃiz]   F
4. [abzɚv]   M
5. [bɪznɪs]   M
6. [nazəl]   M
7. [prɛzɪnt]   M
8. [ɪz]   F
9. [siʒɚ]
10. [babslɛdz]   F

/z/ Transcription Exercise 6–8
Track: (CD 1, Track 34)

1. ['bɪzi]
2. ['vɪzɪt]
3. ['zɚkan]
4. ['wizəl]
5. [siz]
6. ['zɪnijə]
7. [ðoz]
8. ['zukini]
9. [gɪvz]

/s/ and /z/ Crossword Puzzle

Across
3. [zɪp]
4. [sɪzəl]
5. [soldʒɚ]

Down
1. [sups]
2. [zil]
3. [zoro]
5. [sizənz]

Fricative Consonant Transcription Exercise 6–9
Track: (CD 1, Track 35)

1. ['fɛstɪv]
2. [swɪs]
3. ['vɛsəl]
4. ['fænsɪfʊl]
5. ['mizəlz]
6. [zɛst]
7. ['vɪvɪd]
8. ['ɛkspɛnsɪv]
9. ['bɪznɪsɪz]
10. [for'gɪv]
11. ['sopsʌdz]
12. ['fæsɪn]
13. [skwiz]
14. ['sɪzɚz]
15. ['farməsi]
16. ['stivɪn]
17. [vaɪs]
18. ['swɪtzɚlænd]
19. ['sefti]
20. [sɪ'vɪljən]

/θ/ I-M-F Table Transcription Exercise 6–10
Track: (CD 1, Track 36)

1. [ɛnθuzijæst]   M
2. [θɚzde]   I
3. [θɪðɚ]   I
4. [ilɪzʌbɛθ]   F
5. [θɚtiθɚd]   I & M
6. [gɑθɪk]   M
7. [kʌθidrəl]   M
8. [θru]   I
9. [ænɪsθiʒʌ]   M
10. [zinɪθ]   F

/θ/ Transcription Exercise 6–11
Track: (CD 1, Track 37)

1. [θɪn]
2. ['bɚθde]
3. [wɪdθ]
4. [tiθ]
5. [θro]
6. ['ɪniθɪŋ]
7. [norθ]
8. ['nʌθɪŋ]
9. [θɔ]

/ð/ I-M-F Table Transcription Exercise 6–12
Track: (CD 1, Track 38)

1. [ðɛm]   I
2. [kloð]   F
3. [hɛðɚ]   M
4. [rɪðəm]   M
5. [tiθ]

6. [nɔrθ]
7. [wɛðɚ]   M
8. [θaɪ]
9. [nɔrðɚn]   M
10. [wɛðɚ]   M

/ð/ Transcription Exercise 6–13
Track: (CD 1, Track 39)

1. [ðɪs]
2. ['iðɚ]
3. [ðɛr]
4. ['faðɚ]
5. [sɪð]
6. [ðo]
7. ['mʌðɚ]
8. [tɪð]
9. [smuð]

"th" Transcription Exercise 6–14
Track: (CD 1, Track 40)

1. ð	11. ð	21. θ
2. ð	12. θ	22. θ
3. θ	13. θ	23. θ
4. θ	14. ð	24. ð
5. ð	15. ð	25. θ
6. ð	16. θ	26. ð
7. θ	17. ð	27. ð
8. ð	18. ð	28. ð
9. θ	19. ð	29. ð
10. ð	20. θ	30. θ

/θ/ and /ð/ Crossword Puzzle

Across
1. [faðɚ]
2. [ðoz]
3. [mʌðɚz]
4. [θɪn]
6. [rɪðəm]

Down
1. [fɛðɚz]
3. [mɛθadɪk]
5. [nɔrθ]

Interdental Consonant Transcription Exercise 6–15
Track: (CD 1, Track 41)

1. [baɪk'ʌθɔn]
2. [wadz'wɚθ]
3. [saʊθɪstɚn]
4. ['ʌrɪθmətɪk]
5. [sɛvəntinθ]
6. ['θrɛtɪn]
7. [ʌndɚgroθ]
8. [sʌðɚnmost]
9. [θʌndɚ'bɚd]
10. ['plɪməθ]

11. [ruθlɛsli]
12. [wɪðɚspun]
13. ['hartθrab]
14. ['wɚði]
15. ['θraɪvɪŋ]
16. [ən'ʌðɚ]
17. [mɛθadɪk]
18. ['θaʔlɛs]
19. ['hʌndrɛθ]
20. ['lɛðɚ]

/h/ Transcription Exercise 6–16
Track: (CD 1, Track 42)

1. [hum]   I
2. [rihɚs]   M
3. [hɪtʃhaɪk]   I & M
4. [ʌnholsəm]   M
5. [hoze]   I
6. [ɪnhel]   M
7. [hɪləmanstɚ]   I
8. [hæbɪtæt]   I
9. [mʌhagəni]   M
10. [ɛkshəleʃən]   M

/h/ Transcription Exercise 6–17
Track: (CD 1, Track 43)

1. [hɛft]
2. ['harbɚ]
3. [mo'hɛr]
4. ['ʌphɪl]
5. [hʌm]
6. ['ɪnhɛrɪt]
7. ['rihɚs]
8. ['hɚmɪt]
9. ['ʌnhʊk]

/ʍ/ I-M-F Table Transcription Exercise 6–18
Track: (CD 1, Track 44)

1. [ʍil]   I
2. [kʍin]   M
3. [sʍɛr]   M
4. [ʍaɪ]   I
5. [sʍed]   M
6. [ʍɛr]   I
7. [holʍit]   M
8. [wɛr]
9. [wægɪn]
10. [skʍɛr]   M

/ʍ/ Transcription Exercise 6–19
Track: (CD 1, Track 45)

1. [ʍim]
2. ['ovɚʍɛlm]
3. [ʍɪp]
4. [tʍɛnti]
5. [ʃʍa]
6. [ʍaɪt]
7. ['sʌmʍɛr]
8. ['ʍɛðɚ]
9. [ʍorf]

/h/ and /hw/ Transcription Exercise 6–20
Track: (CD 1, Track 46)

1. [hɛdʒhɑg]	11. [hu]
2. [sʍed]	12. [ʍæmi]
3. [mɝl]	13. [holhɑrtɪd]
4. [hum]	14. [ʍɛr]
5. [sʍe]	15. [pɪnʍil]
6. [wɑhu]	16. [hɪm]
7. [ʍaɪn]	17. [pɝɛsʍed]
8. [hændʃek]	18. [ʍɪsəl]
9. [hɛr]	19. [ohaɪo]
10. [ʍɪf]	20. [huz]

/ʃ/ Transcription Exercise 6–21
Track: (CD 1, Track 47)

1. [kʌndɪʃən]	M
2. [ʌʃɝ]	M
3. [tɪʃju]	M
4. [broʃɝ]	M
5. [ʃɪfɑn]	I
6. [ɪnɪʃəl]	M
7. [trɛʒɝ]	
8. [lɪkorɪʃ]	F
9. [krieʃən]	M
10. [ʃubrʌʃ]	I & F

/ʃ/ Transcription Exercise 6–22
Track: (CD 1, Track 48)

1. [ʃu]
2. ['mʌstæʃ]
3. ['oʃən]
4. ['ɪnʃɝ]
5. [wɪʃ]
6. [ʃɪp]
7. ['rɛlɪʃ]
8. [ʃek]
9. ['fæʃən]

/ʒ/ Transcription Exercise 6–23
Track: (CD 1, Track 49)

1. [vɪʒɪn]	M	Track #
2. [ʌfeʒə]	M	
3. [gʌrɑʒ]	F	
4. [steʃən]		
5. [trɛʒɝ]	M	
6. [pɝʒə]	M	
7. [kloʒɝ]	M	
8. [ruʒ]	F	
9. [kʌmpoʒɝ]	M	
10. [tɛləvɪʒən]	M	

/ʒ/ Transcription Exercise 6–24
Track: (CD 1, Track 50)

1. ['rɛʒim]
2. [loʒ]
3. ['plɛʒɝ]
4. [dɪvɪʒɪn]
5. [juʒuəl]
6. [kʌlɪʒən]
7. [beʒ]
8. ['kolɑʒ]
9. [kæʒuəl]

/ʃ/ and /ʒ/ Crossword Puzzle

Across	Down
1. [vekeʃən]	2. [kʌlɪʒən]
3. [liʒɝ]	5. [fɪʃ]
4. [ʌfeʒə]	
6. [ʃʌn]	

Chapter 7

/tʃ/ Transcription Exercise 7–1
Track: (CD 1, Track 51)

1. [ʃɛf]	
2. [hætʃɪt]	M
3. [pɪtʃ]	F
4. [broʃɝ]	
5. [kord]	
6. [kʌltʃɝ]	M
7. [ek]	
8. [mʌʃin]	
9. [tʃɝtʃ]	I & F
10. [fjutʃɝ]	M

/tʃ/ Transcription Exercise 7–2
Track: (CD 1, Track 52)

1. [tʃɪn]
2. ['pitʃɪz]
3. [wɪtʃ]
4. [tʃiz]
5. [lʌntʃ]
6. ['titʃɝ]
7. ['tʃɪldrɛn]
8. [skatʃ]
9. ['fɝnətʃɝ]

/dʒ/ Transcription Exercise 7–3
Track: (CD 1, Track 53)

1. [gʌradʒ]	F
2. [bʌdʒɪt]	M
3. [dʒɪndʒɝ]	I & M

4. [dʌndʒən]   M
5. [dʒʌmp]   I
6. [ɛdʒjukeʃən]   M
7. [dʒɛstɚ]   I
8. [vɔɪjɪdʒ]   F
9. [ɪndʒin]   M
10. [splɚdʒ]   F

/dʒ/ Transcription Exercise 7–4
Track: (CD 1, Track 54)

1. [dʒʌŋk]
2. [ɛn'dʒɔɪ]
3. [ɚdʒd]
4. ['vidʒəl]
5. [wedʒ]
6. [dʒɛm]
7. ['dʒʌmbo]
8. ['kalədʒɪn]
9. [fʌdʒ]

/tʃ/ and /dʒ/ Crossword Puzzle

Across   Down
2. [endʒəlz]   1. [klɚdʒi]
3. [ridʒɔɪs]   4. [samz]
5. [pritʃɚz]

Fricative and Affricate Consonant Transcription Exercise 7–5
Track: (CD 1, Track 55)

1. ['ʃuʃaɪn]   11. ['stedʒkotʃ]
2. [daɪ'dʒɛstʃn]   12. ['tʃaɪldɪʃ]
3. ['kʌnfjuʒɪn]   13. ['hadʒpadʒ]
4. ['antɚaʒ]   14. [pɛriʒən]
5. [ægrɪ'kʌltʃɚ]   15. ['sʌgdʒɛstʃən]
6. [vaɪ'veʃəs]   16. [tʃɪntʃilə]
7. ['sæbətaʒ]   17. [kolɛkʃən]
8. [ɛn'tʃæntɪd]   18. [fortʃənɪt]
9. [dʒɛk]   19. [bjutɪʃən]
10. [ʃɪptuʃor]   20. [vɪʒjulaɪz]

Chapter 8

/w/ Transcription Exercise 8–1
Track: (CD 1, Track 56)

1. [wʌnts]   I
2. [wɪdo]   I
3. [gwam]   M
4. [twaɪs]   M
5. [ɪgwanə]   M
6. [ʍɛr]
7. [kiwi]   M
8. [kʍɛstʃɪn]

9. [wɪlo]   I
10. [eŋgwɪʃ]   M

/w/ Transcription Exercise 8–2
Track: (CD 1, Track 57)

1. [wæks]
2. ['dʒægwɑr]
3. [bi'wɛr]
4. [swɛl]
5. ['wʌndɚ]
6. [kwin]
7. ['forwɚd]
8. [twɪn]
9. [wɛt]

/j/ Transcription Exercise 8–3
Track: (CD 1, Track 58)

1. [ɪndʒɛkt]
2. [rɔɪjəl]   M
3. [jɛt]   I
4. [zɪljən]   M
5. [bʌnjən]   M
6. [spænjəl]   M
7. [jojo]   I & M
8. [lejɛt]   M
9. [fɪgjɚ]   M
10. [kaɪjoti]   M

/j/ Transcription Exercise 8–4
Track: (CD 1, Track 59)

1. [jor]
2. [bi'jand]
3. [jild]
4. [pʌ'paɪjə]
5. ['jandɚ]
6. [fʌmɪljɚ]
7. [jarn]
8. ['bɪljʌn]
9. [jɛs]

/l/ Transcription Exercise 8–5
Track: (CD 1, Track 60)

1. [mɔl]   F
2. [lɪnolijəm]   I & M
3. [wel]   F
4. [æpəl]   F
5. [fɛlo]   M
6. [kævz]
7. [lʌləbaɪ]   I & M
8. [flotɪlə]   M
9. [hɛlm]   M
10. [soʃəbəl]   F

/l/ Transcription Exercise 8–6
Track: (CD 1, Track 61)

1. ['lʌki]
2. ['lɛmən]
3. [klaʊn]
4. ['sændəl]
5. ['goldən]
6. [ɛls]
7. ['braɪdəl]
8. [fli]
9. ['liɑn]

/r/ Transcription Exercise 8–7
Track: (CD 1, Track 62)

1. [ræp]   I
2. [raɪ]   I
3. [skɑr]   F
4. [riport]   I & M
5. [rʌbɚ]   M
6. [wordrob]   M
7. [raɪ]   I
8. [gardɪn]   M
9. [bifor]   F
10. [dir]   F

/r/ Transcription Exercise 8–8
Track: (CD 1, Track 63)

1. [raɪt]
2. [ɪm'prɛs]
3. [ri'dus]
4. ['sari]
5. [raɪm]
6. ['ɔlrɛdi]
7. [tʃɛr]
8. [rʌb]
9. [bar]

/iɾ/ Transcription Exercise 8–9
Track: (CD 1, Track 64)

1. [spir]   F
2. [wird]   M
3. [siriz]   M
4. [stir]   F
5. [pɛr]   F
6. [firs]   M
7. [irʌ]   I
8. [kʌrir]   F
9. [mɝθ]   M
10. [waɪjɚ]   F

/ɛr/ Transcription Exercise 8–10
Track: (CD 1, Track 65)

1. [ɛr]   I
2. [skwɛr]   F
3. [bɛrəl]   M
4. [wɛr]   F
5. [trelɚ]
6. [ɛr]   I
7. [pɝl]
8. [tʃɛr]   F
9. [bɛr]   F
10. [kɛrəmɛl]   M

/ɑr/ Transcription Exercise 8–11
Track: (CD 1, Track 66)

1. [hɑrt]   M
2. [star]   F
3. [sardʒɪnt]   M
4. [fars]   M
5. [kɛrɪdʒ]
6. [stɛr]
7. [mɛri]
8. [mʌrin]
9. [parti]   M
10. [karbʌn]   M

/or/ Transcription Exercise 8–12
Track: (CD 1, Track 67)

1. [forθ]   M
2. [kʌort]   M
3. [parlɚ]
4. [worf]   M
5. [sor]   F
6. [wort]   M
7. [rumɚ]
8. [kort]   M
9. [por]   F
10. [wɝld]

/j/, /l/, and /r/ Crossword Puzzle

Across
2. [jɛlo]
4. [roz]
5. [dʒʌŋgelgrin]
7. [vaɪolɛt]
8. [mərun]

Down
1. [til]
3. [orɪndʒ]
6. [lævɪndɚ]

Vowel plus r Transcription Exercise 8–13
Track: (CD 1, Track 68)

1. ['ɪrmark]	11. [spɑrs]
2. ['kɛrwɔrn]	12. ['ɑrdvɑrk]
3. [or]	13. [dʒɪr]
4. [spɪrz]	14. [bor]
5. ['kɑrport]	15. ['fɔrskʍɛr]
6. [ʃir]	16. [fɑrs]
7. ['hɑrdwɛr]	17. [kɔrs]
8. [dɑrt]	18. [smɪrz]
9. [fɔr'lɔrn]	19. [stɑrtʃ]
10. [rɛr]	20. [bɛr]

Oral Resonant Consonant
Transcription Exercise 8–14
Track: (CD 1, Track 69)

1. [jok]	11. ['redijetɚ]
2. [dwɔrf]	12. ['kʍaɪjɪtli]
3. [liwe]	13. ['væljɛnt]
4. [domɪnjʌn]	14. ['frikʍɛntsi]
5. ['kʍɪbəl]	15. ['lɔɪjɚ]
6. ['lɑrsɪni]	16. ['wewɚd]
7. [jɚenijəm]	17. ['jolandʌ]
8. [ɪləstret]	18. ['stæljʌnz]
9. ['ræli]	19. ['rɛsəl]
10. ['sɔɪjɚ]	20. [jɔn]

Chapter 10

/i/ Transcription Exercise 10–1
Track: (CD 2, Track 1)

1. [jɛs]	
2. [livɪŋ]	M
3. [il]	I
4. [θivz]	M
5. [pipəl]	M
6. [tʃipɪn]	M
7. [kiʃ]	M
8. [strit]	M
9. [hilɪks]	M
10. [haɪjɚ]	

/i/ Transcription Exercise 10–2
Track: (CD 2, Track 2)

1. [it]
2. [kip]
3. [did]
4. [ki]
5. [bik]
6. [pik]
7. [bit]
8. [ti]
9. [dip]

/ɪ/ Transcription Exercise 10–3
Track: (CD 2, Track 3)

1. [maɪld]	
2. [ɪt]	I
3. [pɪksi]	M
4. [bɪljən]	M
5. [faɪn]	
6. [gɪlt]	M
7. [vɪlɪn]	M
8. [sɪnsiɚ]	M
9. [lɪmpf]	M
10. [fɪn]	M

/ɪ/ Transcription Exercise 10–4
Track: (CD 2, Track 4)

1. [kɪk]
2. [gɪg]
3. [bɪld]
4. [tɪk]
5. [ɪt]
6. [bɪt]
7. [pɪk]
8. [kɪd]
9. [bɪg]

/ɛ/ Transcription Exercise 10–5
Track: (CD 2, Track 5)

1. [ɛntel]	I
2. [pɛŋgwɪn]	M
3. [bɛl]	M
4. [maɪld]	
5. [jɛs]	M
6. [ɛlf]	I
7. [gæŋ]	
8. [ɛθɪk]	I
9. [gɛs]	M
10. [dʒɛləs]	M

/ɛ/ Transcription Exercise 10–6
Track: (CD 2, Track 6)

1. [mɛld]
2. [ɛnd]
3. [dɛl]
4. [dɛn]
5. [lɛd]
6. [nɛl]
7. [dɛnts]
8. [slɛd]
9. [ɛtʃ]

/e/ Transcription Exercise 10–7
Track: (CD 2, Track 7)

1. [ekorn]   I
2. [sle]   F
3. [ven]   M
4. [daɪl]
5. [liʒɚ]
6. [gen]   M
7. [bæg]
8. [le]   F
9. [əten]   M
10. [rendir]   M

/e/ Transcription Exercise 10–8
Track: (CD 2, Track 8)

1. [ves]
2. [stez]
3. [zen]
4. [et]
5. [fez]
6. [test]
7. [fes]
8. [ʃev]
9. [fet]

/æ/ Transcription Exercise 10–9
Track: (CD 2, Track 9)

1. [ædvænts]   I & M
2. [pæn]   M
3. [ænt]   I
4. [mɑl]
5. [pen]
6. [dæmpnɪs]   M
7. [kwæk]   M
8. [kæsked]   M
9. [mæθ]   M
10. [wɛnt]

/æ/ Transcription Exercise 10–10
Track: (CD 2, Track 10)

1. [sæʃ]
2. [fæst]
3. [æʃ]
4. [stæf]
5. [væt]
6. [ʃæft]
7. [tæt]
8. [æz]
9. [sæv]

/i/, /ɪ/, /ɛ/, /e/, /æ/, and /w/ Crossword Puzzle

Across
1. [wɛbstɚ]
2. [wɪnstʌn]
4. [len]
5. [mɛri]

Down
1. [wɪn]
2. [wɪljʌm]
3. [tɪm]
6. [ʃilʌ]

Front Vowel Transcription Exercise 10–11
Track: (CD 2, Track 11)

1. [flem]
2. ['æli]
3. [bi'liv]
4. [re'zɪn]
5. [wik'de]
6. ['rilæks]
7. [æsk]
8. ['pipəl]
9. [rɛmnɪnt]
10. [ren]
11. ['dʒɪmnɪst]
12. ['eprɪn]
13. ['nemsek]
14. ['bɪzi]
15. ['kæfin]
16. ['wɪmɪn]
17. ['hɛdek]
18. [pliz]
19. ['bɪskɪt]
20. ['ɛldɪst]

Chapter 11

/ə/ Transcription Exercise 11–1
Track: (CD 2, Track 12)

1. [əhɛd]   I
2. [rətæn]   M
3. [məʃin]   M
4. [bətɑn]   M
5. [kʌbɑnə]   F
6. [hɛlo]
7. [kʌp]
8. [əgri]   I
9. [bəfe]   M
10. [kəkun]   M

/ə/ Transcription Exercise 11–2
Track: (CD 2, Track 13)

1. [gə'lor]
2. [sə'port]
3. [ə'lon]
4. [kəm'poz]
5. [kən'don]
6. [pə'trol]
7. [rə'por]
8. [ə'poz]
9. ['orəl]

/ə/ Crossword Puzzle

Across
4. [səpoz]
5. [kəkun]
6. [ləgun]

Down
1. [pəpus]
2. [gəzəl]
3. [əpɑn]

/ʌ/ Transcription Exercise 11–3
Track: (CD 2, Track 14)

1. [ʌv]   I
2. [tʃʌg]   M
3. [wʌn]   M
4. [ʌnkʌt]   I & M
5. [wʌz]   M
6. [jʌŋ]   M
7. [rʌst]   M
8. [ʌp]   I
9. [wʌn]   M
10. [rust]

/ʌ/ Transcription Exercise 11–4
Track: (CD 2, Track 15)

1. [ʌv]
2. [tʌtʃ]
3. [θʌm]
4. [wʌz]
5. ['tʌnəl]
6. [pʌn]
7. [mʌt]
8. ['ʃʌvəl]
9. [nʌt]

/ʌ/ Crossword Puzzle

Across	Down
3. [ʌnglud]	1. [dʌst]
6. [ʃʌt]	2. [hʌʃ]
	4. [gʌmbo]
	5. [dʌk]

/ɚ/ Transcription Exercise 11–5
Track: (CD 2, Track 16)

1. [æktɚ]   M
2. [ɝnɚ]   F
3. [nɝd]
4. [ʃʊgɚ]   F
5. [eŋgɚ]   F
6. [nebɚ]   F
7. [kritʃɚ]   F
8. [netʃɚ]   F
9. [glæmɚ]   F
10. [fɚbɪd]   M

/ɚ/ Transcription Exercises 11–6
Track: (CD 2, Track 17)

1. ['netʃɚ]
2. ['medʒɚ]
3. ['bekɚ]
4. ['rezɚ]
5. ['letɚ]
6. ['pesɚ]
7. ['feljɚ]
8. ['nebɚ]
9. ['sefɚ]

/ɚ/ Crossword Puzzle

Across	Down
3. [flaʊwɚ]	1. [ɛvɚ]
4. [læntɚn]	2. [ɛfɚt]
	4. [lidɚ]
	5. [nɛvɚ]

/ɝ/ Transcription Exercise 11–7
Track: (CD 2, Track 18)

1. [ɝb]   M
2. [wɝst]   M
3. [slɝ]   F
4. [tʃɝp]   M
5. [sevɚ]
6. [ɝn]   I
7. [fitʃɝ]   F
8. [ɝn]   I
9. [tɝtəl]   M
10. [mɝtəl]   M

/ɝ/ Transcription Exercise 11–8
Track: (CD 2, Track 19)

1. [ɝdʒ]
2. [vɝb]
3. [bɝθ]
4. [θɝd]
5. [dɝdʒ]
6. [bɝ]
7. [gɝθ]
8. [dʒɝm]
9. [ɝθ]

/ɝ/ Crossword Puzzle

Across	Down
2. [ɝbəl]	1. [bɝst]
4. [θɝsti]	3. [zɝkan]
6. [nɝsmed]	5. [θɝd]

Central Vowels Transcription Exercise 11–9
Track: (CD 2, Track 20)

1. [hæmbɚgɚ]	11. ['tɝnɚ]
2. [sʌdz]	12. [kʌn'fɝm]
3. [kɝn]	13. ['bʌzɚ]
4. ['kʌvɚ]	14. ['mʌtʃɚ]
5. [ʌ'kɚ]	15. ['bʌfɚ]

6. [ˈfɝ·və]   16. [tʃɝp]
7. [ˈʌndʌn]   17. [sɝ·dʒ]
8. [ˈirdrʌm]   18. [vɝs]
9. [ˈmɝ·mɝ]   19. [sʌbˈmɝ·dʒ]
10. [əˈwaɪl]   20. [ˈmɝ·dʒɝ]

Chapter 12

/u/ Transcription Exercise 12–1
Track: (CD 2, Track 21)

1. [nudəl]   M
2. [du]   F
3. [du]   F
4. [ʃʊd]
5. [uz]   I
6. [sut]   M
7. [butik]   M
8. [ful]   M
9. [duk]   M
10. [tu]   F

/u/ Transcription Exercise 12–2
Track: (CD 2, Track 22)

1. [rul]
2. [su]
3. [lus]
4. [ru]
5. [lup]
6. [flu]
7. [slup]
8. [pul]
9. [ful]

/ʊ/ Transcription Exercise 12–3
Track: (CD 2, Track 23)

1. [fʊl]   M
2. [ʊps]   I
3. [wʊlf]   M
4. [mʌt]
5. [sʊt]   M
6. [guf]
7. [wʊps]   M
8. [ʃʊgɝ]   M
9. [fʊtstul]   M
10. [hʊd]   M

/ʊ/ Transcription Exercise 12–4
Track: (CD 2, Track 24)

1. [kʊk]
2. [wʊl]
3. [fʊt]
4. [wʊd]

5. [lʊk]
6. [wʊlf]
7. [fʊl]
8. [kʊd]
9. [nʊk]

/o/ Transcription Exercise 12–5
Track: (CD 2, Track 25)

1. [old]   I
2. [mut]
3. [so]   F
4. [loʃən]   M
5. [mo]   F
6. [hu]
7. [kolə]   M
8. [tost]   M
9. [bol]   M
10. [matʃo]   F

/o/ Transcription Exercise 12–6
Track: (CD 2, Track 26)

1. [not]
2. [ton]
3. [on]
4. [tot]
5. [no]
6. [ot]
7. [hon]
8. [no]
9. [o]

/ɔ/ Transcription Exercise 12–7
Track: (CD 2, Track 27)

1. [ɔl]   I
2. [θɔŋ]   M
3. [sɔs]   M
4. [ɔ]   I
5. [ʃwɔ]   F
6. [mɔθ]   M
7. [pɔ]   F
8. [skwɔ]   F
9. [pɔ]   F
10. [θɔt]   M

/ɔ/ Transcription Exercise 12–8
Track: (CD 2, Track 28)

1. [sɔt]
2. [ˈbɔdi]
3. [rɔt]
4. [prɔn]
5. [kɔl]

6. [brɔd]
7. [θɔt]
8. [vɔlt]
9. [ʌnˈlɔfʊl]

/ɑ/ Transcription Exercise 12–9
Track: (CD 2, Track 29)

1. [past̬ə]   M
2. [amənd]   I
3. [spɑ]   F
4. [lantʃ]   M
5. [ʒɑnrə]   M
6. [jat]   M
7. [ɑkwə]   I
8. [lʌntʃ]
9. [ʃwɑ]   F
10. [antre]   I

/ɑ/ Transcription Exercise 12–10
Track: (CD 2, Track 30)

1. [ɑ]
2. [nat]
3. [hɑ]
4. [jat]
5. [tat]
6. [jan]
7. [hant]
8. [tat]
9. [ant]

/u/, /ʊ/, /o/, /ɔ/, and /ɑ/ Crossword Puzzle

Across
3. [ɔfʊl]
5. [lɔŋ]
6. [to]
7. [sok]

Down
1. [θɔŋ]
2. [fʊt]
4. [lo]
5. [lus]

Back Vowel Transcription Exercise 12–11
Track: (CD 2, Track 31)

1. [ˈkupan]
2. [hʊk]
3. [ˈankor]
4. [hɑˈθorn]
5. [ˈnuzrum]
6. [ˈtako]
7. [ˈjojo]
8. [ˈɔfʊl]
9. [jat]
10. [lalipap]
11. [ˈkʊkbʊk]
12. [ˈbostfʊl]
13. [ˈfʊtstul]
14. [ˈhorsʃu]
15. [fɔt]
16. [ˈdormrum]
17. [frut]
18. [ˈmɑθbɔl]
19. [sok]
20. [ˈθɔtfʊl]

Chapter 13

/aɪ/ Transcription Exercise 13–1
Track: (CD 2, Track 32)

1. [aɪlɪnd]   I
2. [aɪ]   I
3. [gaɪ]   F
4. [maɪnəs]   M
5. [daɪl]   M
6. [raɪm]   M
7. [swit]
8. [haɪ]   F
9. [nis]
10. [braɪd]   M

/aɪ/ Transcription Exercise 13–2
Track: (CD 2, Track 33)

1. [baɪ]
2. [ˈsaɪdɚ]
3. [haɪt]
4. [ˈfaɪsti]
5. [slaɪs]
6. [taɪm]
7. [raɪt]
8. [saɪ]
9. [raɪm]

/aʊ/ Transcription Exercise 13–3
Track: (CD 2, Track 34)

1. [aʊtʃ]   I
2. [lan]
3. [kaʊwɚd]   M
4. [vaʊwəl]   M
5. [haʊ]   F
6. [tafi]
7. [ʃaʊt]   M
8. [no]
9. [laʊndʒ]   M
10. [haʊs]   M

/aʊ/ Transcription Exercise 13–4
Track: (CD 2, Track 35)

1. [aʊst]
2. [traʊt]
3. [ˈgaʊdʒɪŋ]
4. [praʊwəl]
5. [ˈtʃaʊdɚ]
6. [ˈhaʊshold]
7. [baʊnd]
8. [laʊs]
9. [baʊ]

/ɔɪ/ Transcription Exercise 13–5
Track: (CD 2, Track 36)

1. [kɔɪ]   F
2. [tʃɔɪs]   M
3. [taʊn]
4. [dʒɔɪn]   M
5. [saɪfɚ]
6. [mɔɪst]   M
7. [mɪst]
8. [bɔɪjent]   M
9. [dʒus]
10. [spɔɪl]   M

/ɔɪ/ Transcription Exercise 13–6
Track: (CD 2, Track 37)

1. ['hɔɪstɪŋ]
2. ['kɔɪld]
3. ['dɛstrɔɪ]
4. [fɔɪlz]
5. ['lɔɪtɚ]
6. ['vɔɪsɪŋ]
7. [tɔɪ]
8. [ɛks'plɔɪt]
9. [ə'vɔɪd]

/ju/ Transcription Exercise 13–7
Track: (CD 2, Track 38)

1. [fju]   F
2. [junjən]   I
3. [bjuti]   M
4. [kjut]   M
5. [pju]   F
6. [juz]   I
7. [hjudʒ]   M
8. [ful]
9. [hjumɚ]   M
10. [hulə]

/ju/ Transcription Exercise 13–8
Track: (CD 2, Track 39)

1. [ju]
2. ['fjuʃə]
3. ['mjuzɪk]
4. [hjudʒ]
5. ['mjutɪnt]
6. ['pjupəl]
7. [spjud]
8. [bjut]
9. [fjum]

Diphthong Crossword Puzzle

Across	Down
1. [mɔɪst]	1. [mju]
3. [kju]	2. [spɔɪld]
4. [daʊn]	5. [naʊn]
6. [naɪn]	7. [aɪsaɪt]

Diphthong Transcription Exercise 13–9
Track: (CD 2, Track 40)

1. ['faʊndri]   11. [paʊt]
2. [dʒɔɪn]   12. [baɪt]
3. ['jukɑn]   13. [naʊn]
4. [braɪn]   14. [nɔɪz]
5. [tɔɪl]   15. ['fraʊnɪŋ]
6. [dʒænjuwɛri]   16. [aɪ]
7. [aʊst]   17. [kʌntrɪbjutɚ]
8. ['jukəleli]   18. [ɔɪŋk]
9. [mɔɪst]   19. [maɪm]
10. ['æmjulɛt]   20. ['braʊniz]

Chapter 15

Transcription Exercise 15–1
Track: (CD 2, Track 41)

1. [fɪkst]   11. ['fregrænts]
2. ['kæntsəl]   12. ['stʌmɪks]
3. [stɑpːʊʃɪŋ]   13. [kɪs'ɝ]
4. [dʒʌŋk]   14. ['kʌmpfɚt]
5. [pʊʃt]   15. [blæk:orn]
6. [drɛmpt]   16. [bʌgz]
7. [go'we]   17. [lɛmigo]
8. [wɪgz]   18. [prɪnts]
9. [mɪŋk]   19. [sidz]
10. [lɪtəlːusi]   20. [θɪnːaɪf]

Chapter 4 Word Search #1: /p/ and /b/

```
s  ʃ  r  d  aɪ p  ɚ  z  d  ɔ  l  t  z  r
dʒ ɚ  k  ʃ  ə  b  p  æ  n  d  ə  ð  ʌ
b  a  t  ə  l  o  r  r  i  æ  k  n  ʊ  d
s  tʃ i  w  b  l  u  p  m  ɪ  p  z  n  kʍ
h  p  ɛ  t  e  v  i  b  b  e  u  l  m  p
f  a  ʒ  ŋ  b  ɛ  ʌ  ɔ  k  r  ɪ  p  t  s
k  p  t  θ  i  p  z  z  t  dʒ i  b  v  n
l  a  s  l  z  ŏ  w  k  m  æ  ʒ  n  æ  p
b  ɛ  f  o  ɪ  ɛ  r  ʃ  ɪ  k  o  u  r  æ
h  b  æ  s  ɪ  n  ɛ  t  r  g  l  ʊ  f  s
n  ɪ  z  ɛ  g  ɪ  ʌ  i  d  r  s  n  ɪ
s  b  e  b  ɪ  b  n  z  b  ʌ  n  i  g  f
p  ɪ  ŋ  k  w  dʒ ŏ  b  e  ʌ  ɛ  ɪ  ʒ  aɪ
j  f  eɪ w  ə  p  r  ɝ  g  v  z  j
l  b  l  æ  ŋ  k  ɛ  t  p  t  d  i  ɔ  ɚ
r  g  h  p  ks f  m  ɚ  b  g  a  r  ə  g
```

Chapter 4 Word Search #2: /t/, /d/, /k/, and /g/

```
g  u  o  t  aɪ m  b  k  ʌ  v  l  ɛ  k  t
k  ɔ  v  i  r  n  ʌ  t  m  ɛ  g  n  g  d
e  ʌ  d  ð  ɚ  ʒ  w  z  s  f  j  c  t  ʃ
p  k  ɛ  k  i  k  j  u  m  ɪ  n  h  ʒ  ɝ  o
ɚ  w  s  ə  ʌ  æ  ə  c  h  l  e  h  m  ɚ  ɛ
z  i  o  l  t  k  f  u  d  o  ɛ  m  ɚ  ʌ
e  k  ɛ  r  o  w  e  r  ɪ  t  ð  ɪ  ʌ
h  s  r  æ  r  k  d  k  l  p  p  o  k  θ
k  f  t  k  ɛ  ɛ  v  m  t  r  t  l  p  n
r  k  m  d  g  r  k  ɔ  r  i  æ  n  d  ɚ
g  ɝ  æ  v  ə  t  r  o  ŋ  h  ɪ  t  b  m
b  i  ð  r  n  θ  p  æ  p  r  i  k  ə  g
o  ɪ  ɛ  k  o  g  t  n  ð  e  ʒ  æ  v  r
w  n  k  l  o  v  z  h  e  v  d  ɛ  g  j
f  tʃ z  i  u  n  t  ɛ  r  ə  g  a  n  ə
k  a  r  d  ə  m  ə  m  ɛ  n  æ  t  tʃ t
```

Chapter 5 Word Search #3: /m/ and /n/

```
m  e  m  æ  g  n  o  l  j  ə  l  n
d  o  ə  p  k  d  ʒ  i  e  ɪ  z  ɛ
ɛ  f  o  r  dʒ u  ʌ  p  ɛ  u  ŋ  r
l  r  ð  ɪ  n  n  s  i  ɪ  o  p  v
f  s  m  m  ʌ  m  t  t  u  o  æ  θ
ɪ  p  ʃ  r  j  v  ks u  ʊ  ɝ  n  g
n  b  t  o  d  f  k  n  b  ɚ  z  o
i  t  ɪ  z  e  p  a  i  i  ə  i  k
ə  d  s  o  m  ɛ  r  ə  g  o  l  d
m  k  r  p  i  o  n  i  o  ʌ  s  h
ə  g  u  z  tʃ w  e  ʒ  n  k  s  ʒ
dʒ æ  z  m  i  n  ʃ  z  i  g  z  z
j  w  ɔ  ɪ  æ  n  ə  e  ə  s  r  v
ʌ  z  ɪ  n  i  ə  n  w  o  z  w  f
```

Chapter 5 Word Search #4: /ŋ/

```
ʃ  d  l  ɔ  p  n  b  ʌ  dʒ ʃ  ɪ  r  ʒ
æ  ŋ  k  ɚ  r  k  z  æ  ɝ  j  ɝ  ɛ  o
d  s  d  ʒ  θ  tʃ ɪ  d  c  k  ɚ
ɪ  a  n  ʒ  ɔ  ʌ  r  m  r  h  ɛ  t  k
k  j  æ  ŋ  k  ɪ  ŋ  b  ɪ  e  æ  b
d  t  k  d  ɪ  ŋ  t  s  ŋ  o  l  ŋ  ɪ
ɪ  m  m  ʃ  ə  s  i  ɪ  k  ə  b  g  e
s  l  ɪ  ŋ  ɚ  m  tʃ ə  i  z  ə  w
ŋ  k  ə  w  n  z  w  ʃ  e  tʃ d  l  i
ʃ  l  ɪ  n  i  k  m  ʌ  ŋ  k  n  ð  æ
l  ɛ  h  ŏ  l  o  d  r  l  ɛ  s  t
ʃ  ŋ  l  o  ɪ  l  æ  e  e  o  d  ɛ  l
æ  k  m  tʃ ŋ  g  b  s  w  ɪ  ŋ  z  i
p  θ  r  z  k  n  θ  ɪ  i  u  tʃ d  z
h  ɪ  s  s  ʒ  s  r  ŋ  m  n  r  k  ɪ
```

Chapter 6 Word Search #5: /f/ and /v/

```
v  ɪ  k  t  ɔ  r  i  h  e  d  ɪ  n
m  h  ɛ  g  d  e  t  r  r  b  s  h
ɑ  r  r  ɪ  t  ə  m  ɛ  ɪ  n  k  ɛ
r  ɛ  ə  v  ɪ  n  s  k  s  ɑ  k  p
s  f  ʊ  t  b  ɔ  l  i  i  l  ɪ  d
u  ɚ  n  d  h  ɑ  r  v  i  k  ə
n  i  ə  s  e  f  t  i  ɚ  t  ɔ  h
b  l  u  d  w  ɪ  v  g  u  f  æ
f  ʊ  l  b  æ  k  l  a  m  p  r  f
r  w  f  a  d  s  w  r  θ  ɛ  e  b
ʊ  u  i  dʒ d  ə  ʃ  s  ɛ  r  n  æ
k  d  l  u  æ  m  æ  ɪ  r  i  i  k
s  b  d  l  i  t  m  t  i  dʒ ɛ  r
ɔ  f  ɛ  n  s  a  d  i  f  ɛ  n  s
```

Chapter 6 Word Search #7: /θ/ and /ð/

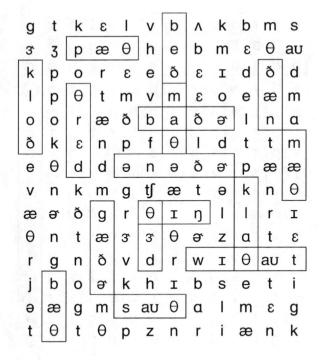

```
g  t  k  ɛ  l  v  b  ʌ  k  b  m  s
ɝ  ʒ  p  æ  θ  h  e  b  m  ɛ  θ  aʊ
k  p  o  r  ɛ  e  ð  ɛ  ɪ  d  ð  d
l  p  θ  t  m  v  m  ɛ  o  e  æ  m
o  o  r  æ  ð  b  a  ð  ɚ  l  n  ɑ
ð  k  ɛ  n  p  f  θ  l  d  t  t  m
e  θ  d  d  ə  n  ə  ð  ɚ  p  æ  æ
v  n  k  m  g  tʃ æ  t  ə  k  n  θ
æ  ɚ  ð  g  r  θ  ɪ  ŋ  l  l  r  ɪ
θ  n  t  æ  ɝ  ʒ  θ  ɚ  z  a  t  ɛ
r  g  n  ð  v  d  r  w  ɪ  θ  aʊ t
j  b  o  ɚ  k  h  ɪ  b  s  e  t  i
ə  æ  g  m  s  aʊ θ  ɑ  l  m  ɛ  g
t  θ  t  θ  p  z  n  r  i  æ  n  k
```

Chapter 6 Word Search #6: /s/ and /z/

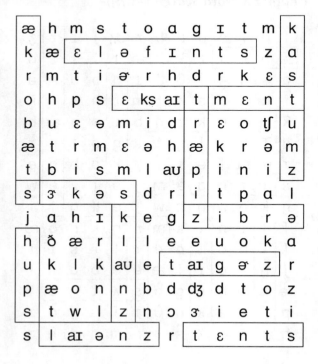

```
æ  h  m  s  t  o  a  g  ɪ  t  m  k
k  æ  ɛ  ə  f  ɪ  n  t  s  z  ɑ
r  m  t  i  ɚ  r  h  d  r  k  ɛ  s
o  h  p  s  ɛ  ks aɪ t  m  ɛ  n  t
b  u  ɛ  ə  m  i  d  r  ɛ  o  tʃ u
æ  t  r  m  ɛ  ə  h  æ  k  r  ə  m
t  b  i  s  m  l  aʊ p  i  n  i  z
s  ɝ  k  ə  s  d  r  i  t  p  a  l
j  ɑ  h  ɪ  k  e  g  z  i  b  r  ə
h  ð  ɚ  r  l  l  e  e  u  o  k  a
u  k  l  k  aʊ e  t  aɪ g  ɚ  z  r
p  æ  o  n  n  b  d  dʒ d  t  o  z
s  t  w  l  z  n  ɔ  ɝ  i  e  t  i
s  l  aɪ ə  n  z  r  t  ɛ  n  t  s
```

Chapter 6 Word Search #8: /ʃ/ and /ʒ/

```
ʃ  æ  l  o  k  ʃ  s  z  n  æ  aɪ p
d  d  d  p  r  r  ɪ  ɪ  k  n  g  ɔ
ɪ  l  ʌ  æ  o  ɪ  t  k  θ  o  l  ə
k  n  k  n  j  m  i  l  ɪ  ʃ  k  ə
d  r  m  ʃ  ɪ  p  s  s  ŋ  r  n  i
ɪ  a  ə  d  u  r  m  l  s  n  ɑ  ʒ
n  s  n  d  t  f  ɪ  ʃ  k  r  ɝ  ə
ʃ  o  l  e  θ  e  ð  ɔ  o  u  j  k
i  m  m  l  w  z  ʃ  ə  l  ʃ  æ  d
ʃ  a  r  k  d  i  l  ə  h  w  b  o
l  i  s  p  r  o  n  ð  n  ɛ  r  l
æ  t  r  ɛ  ʒ  ɚ  tʃ ɛ  s  t  t  æ
p  m  k  l  æ  m  ʃ  ɛ  l  b  m  b
h  ɪ  tʃ u  o  d  ɔ  e  s  ɚ  ʒ
d  k  ɪ  z  b  ʌ  r  l  ɛ  m  n  r
```

Chapter 7 Word Search #9: /tʃ/ and /dʒ/

Chapter 8 Word Search #11: Vowel + r

Chapter 8 Word Search #10: /w/

Chapter 8 Word Search #12: /j/, /l/, and /r/

Chapter 10 Word Search #13: Front Vowels

v g e h k g r i b o w k
f ɪ n p i k ɑ k z v m z
l i p w ʌ tʃ ɪ k ə d i ɔ
o g ɛ ʃ b ə l d f ɛ v u
t ə r o m s e ɛ g s g r
p l ə ɛ t f g n d o ə k
i ð k ɚ l æ k d v r ʃ i
r ɝ i ʌ b l u dʒ e t j w
ɛ r t θ k k dʒ s r m ɝ i
n i n n æ ə tʃ ɪ t æ ɛ s
ɔ n g m o n n ə w g ə f
ʒ e r l j h e ɛ ð p t ɪ
h i g r ɛ t z d r aɪ ŋ n
m ɪ o l ɪ t v i ə i i tʃ

Chapter 12 Word Search #15: Back Vowels

s ʃ r ɑ dʒ ɚ d ɔ l t r i z v m f kʍ
d ʒ ɚ k j u ə b ɑ ɑ z ð ʌ ɝ ɑ n ɪ
b ʌ dʒ ɔ z j o r ɑ r i r ɛ v æ ʌ k
ʊ k p s θ i s ɑ ɛ t æ ɪ w m n u d
l r ɛ k h n dʒ b u g s z ð e d o r
w ʌ p z s u z ɪ n l u tʃ i w p m ɔ
ɪ p v t ð i z n z ɪ l o p h ɑ d m
ŋ æ k s ʃ u kʍ h f n v ɛ o b k f ɑ
k s g t o θ p u m p ʒ o p s ɛ ɪ g
l ɪ u æ l j h d u g ŋ m n p t l r
b w f e w o k ʍ tʃ ɪ o u e i l z ɔ
h ɑ i ə ʌ g ɑ r θ b r u k s o g s
n k w tʃ æ z ʌ z h t w b v u n ʒ d
s kʍ ɪ k d r o m ə g r o j h i g t
j r u p ɔ l ɚ f e ɝ b f dʒ u w e l
l ks ɪ dʒ o r dʒ b u ʃ t s f z r s n

Chapter 11 Word Search #14: /ɚ/ and /ɝ/

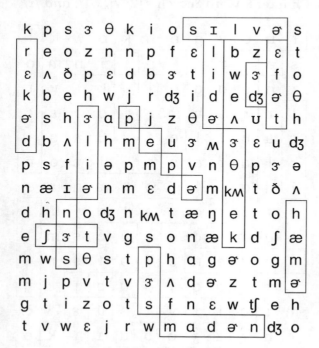

k p s ʒ θ k i o s ɪ l v ɚ s
r e o z n n p f ɛ l b z ɛ t
ɛ ʌ ð p ɛ d b ɝ t i w ɝ f o
k b e h w j r dʒ i d e dʒ ɚ θ
ɚ s h ɝ ɑ p j z θ ɚ ʌ ʊ t h
d b ʌ l h m e u ɝ ʍ ɝ ɛ u dʒ
p s f i ə e p m p v n θ p ɝ ə
n æ ɪ ə n m ɛ d ɚ m kʍ t ð ʌ
d h̃ n o dʒ n kʍ t æ ŋ e t o h
e ʃ ɝ t v g s o n æ k d ʃ æ
m w s θ s t p h a g ɚ o g m
m j p v t v ɝ ʌ d ə z t m ɚ
g t i z o t s f n ɛ w tʃ e h
t v w ɛ j r w m a d ɚ n dʒ o

Chapter 13 Word Search #16: Diphthongs

s ʃ r d o n p ɚ r ɔ t t v
h aɪ æ k s v j u z p n ə ʌ
d s t ə ɛ o ɛ b ɔɪ n r d
b h i n b w w r b s z f k
s aʊ ɛ t k z ʌ u u t i h p
h s aʊ θ b aʊ n d m ɚ b j u s
f p ʒ m ɪ g z i m ʒ u m n
k æ w aɪ l d f aʊ l æ ʊ ɚ p
l ɛ t n æ k h ʌ ɪ k s n æ
b b s θ p ə r z d p i g s
h ɪ f ŋ s ɔɪ l v z ɔɪ v ʒ z
n ju æ l ks dʒ t ʃ e z i z f
s b z f ju ʃ ə t r w ɔ aɪ
o ɪ k aʊ tʃ g j r æ m ə ɚ j

Index

Flash Cards

#1
Voiceless Lingua-Velar Stop-Consonant /k/

Initial	cab	[kæb]
Medial	acorn	[ekorn]
Final	fake	[fek]

#2
Voiced Lingua-Velar Stop-Consonant /g/

Initial	game	[gem]
Medial	begin	[bi'gɪn]
Final	mug	['mʌg]

#3
Voiceless Bilabial Stop-Consonant /p/

Initial	paid	[ped]
Medial	repeat	[ri'pit]
Final	lamp	['læmp]

#4
Voiced Bilabial Stop-Consonant /b/

Initial	burn	['bɝn]
Medial	habit	['hæbɪt]
Final	probe	[prob]

#5
Voiceless Lingua-Alveolar Stop-Consonant /t/

Initial	tea	['ti]
Medial	material	[mə'tiriəl]
Final	cot	[kat]

#6
Voiced Lingua-Alveolar Stop-Consonant /d/

Initial	drop	[drɑp]
Medial	radar	[redar]
Final	yard	[jard]

#7
Voiceless Lingua-Alveolar Fricative /s/

Initial	same	[sem]
Medial	missing	[mɪsɪŋ]
Final	cuffs	[kʌfs]

#8
Voiced Lingua-Alveolar Fricative /z/

Initial	zone	[zon]
Medial	pansy	[pænzi]
Final	clams	[klæmz]

#9
Voiceless Labiodental Fricative /f/

Initial	fern	[fɝn]
Medial	coffee	['kafi]
Final	wife	[waɪf]

f

z

s

p

t

b

p

g

k

#10
Voiced Labiodental Fricative /v/

Initial — verb — [vɝb]

Medial — envy — [ɛnvi]

Final — eve — [iv]

#11
Voiceless Interdental Fricative /θ/

Initial — thick — [θɪk]

Medial — toothpaste — [tuθpest]

Final — booth — [buθ]

#12
Voiced Interdental Fricative /ð/

Initial — then — [ðɛn]

Medial — gather — [gæˈðɚ]

Final — bathe — [beð]

#13
Voiceless Lingua-Palatal Fricative /ʃ/

Initial — shake — [ʃek]

Medial — fishing — [fɪʃɪŋ]

Final — rush — [rʌʃ]

#14
Voiced Lingua-Palatal Fricative /ʒ/

Initial — Does not exist in SAE

Medial — leisure — [liʒɚ]

Final — beige — [beʒ]

#15
Voiceless Glottal Fricative /h/

Initial — ham — [hæm]

Medial — inhale — [ɪnhel]

Final — Does not exist in SAE

#16
Voiceless Labial-Velar Fricative /hw/

Initial — whirl — [ˈhwɝəl]

Medial — buckwheat — [ˈbʌkhwit]

Final — Does not exist in isolation in SAE

#17
Voiceless Alveopalatal Affricate /tʃ/

Initial — chirp — [tʃɝp]

Medial — future — [ˈfjutʃɚ]

Final — research — [riˈsɝtʃ]

#18
Voiced Alveopalatal Affricate /dʒ/

Initial — gel — [dʒɛl]

Medial — magic — [mædʒɪk]

Final — package — [pækɪdʒ]

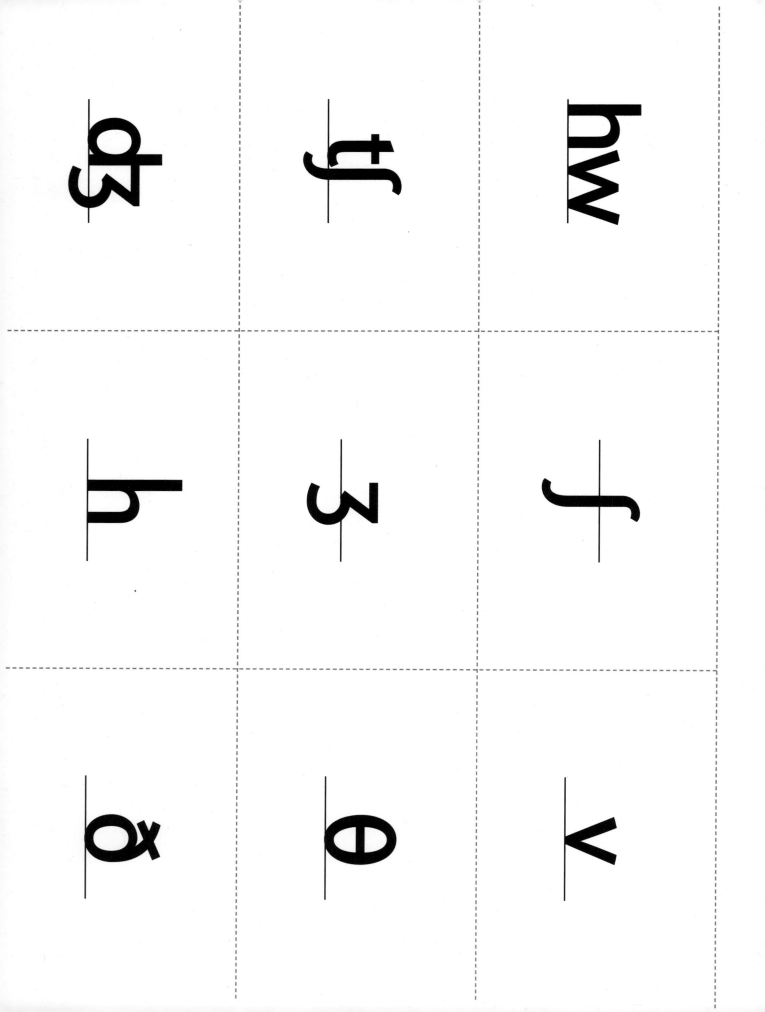

dʒ

tʃ

hw

h

ʒ

f

ð

θ

v

#19 Voiced Bilabial Nasal /m/

Initial: *m*arsh [**m**ɑrʃ]
Medial: co*m*edy [kɑ**m**ɛdi]
Final: alar*m* [ʌlɑr**m**]

#20 Voiced Lingua-Alveolar Nasal /n/

Initial: *n*ear [**n**ir]
Medial: ca*n*al [kʌ**n**æl]
Final: pelica*n* [pɛlɪk**n**]

#21 Voiced Velar Nasal /ŋ/

Initial: Does not exist in SAE
Medial: fi*ng*er [fɪ**ŋ**gɚ]
Final: aski*ng* [æskɪ**ŋ**]

#22 Voiced Lingua-Alveolar Lateral Liquid /l/

Initial: *l*eaf [**l**if]
Medial: do*ll*ar [dɑ**l**ɚ]
Final: scanda*l* [skændə**l**]

#23 Voiced Lingua-Palatal On-Glide /j/

Initial: *y*ogurt [**j**ogɚt]
Medial: ka*y*ak [ka**j**æk]
Final: Does not exist in SAE

#24 Voiced Alveo-Palatal Liquid (Glide) /r/

Initial: *r*aid [**r**ed]
Medial: fab*r*ic [fæb**r**ɪk]
Final: ca*r* [ka**r**]

#25 Voiced Bilabial (Lingua-Velar) Glide /w/

Initial: *w*est [**w**ɛst]
Medial: re*w*ard [ri**w**ord]
Final: Does not exist in SAE

#26 High Front Tense Unrounded Vowel /i/

Initial: *e*ast [**i**st]
Medial: b*ee*f [b**i**f]
Final: m*e* [m**i**]

#27 High Front Lax Unrounded Vowel /ɪ/

Initial: *i*n [**ɪ**n]
Medial: f*i*nish [f**ɪ**nɪʃ]
Final: c*i*ty [sɪt**ɪ**]

Note: The /ɪ/ in SAE occurs in words ending in "y."

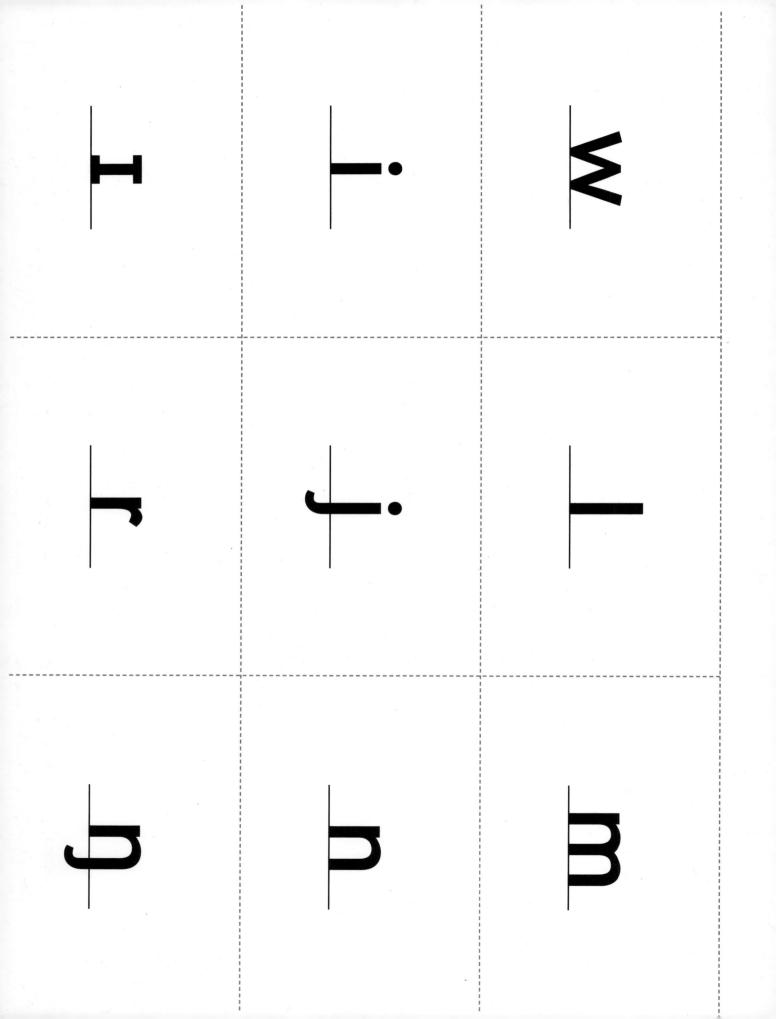

#28
Mid Front Lax Unrounded Vowel /ɛ/

Position	Word	Transcription
Initial	echo	[ˈɛko]
Medial	dent	[ˈdɛnt]
Final	Does not exist in SAE	

#29
Mid-Front Tense Unrounded Vowel /e/

Position	Word	Transcription
Initial	aim	[ˈem]
Medial	bake	[ˈbek]
Final	way	[ˈwe]

#30
Low Front Lax Unrounded Vowel /æ/

Position	Word	Transcription
Initial	at	[ˈæt]
Medial	hatrack	[ˈhætræk]
Final	Does not exist in SAE	

#31
Mid-Central Lax Unrounded Vowel (Unstressed) (Schwa) /ə/

Position	Word	Transcription
Initial	amuse	[əˈmjuz]
Medial	ravine	[rəˈvin]
Final	sofa	[ˈsofə]

#32
Mid-Central Unrounded Vowel (Stressed) /ʌ/

Position	Word	Transcription
Initial	oven	[ˈʌvin]
Medial	bumpy	[ˈbʌmpi]
Final	Does not exist in SAE	

#33
Mid-Central R-Colored Lax Vowel (Unstressed) /ɚ/

Position	Word	Transcription
Initial	urbane	[ɚˈben]
Medial	scattering	[ˈskætɚɪŋ]
Final	mayor	[ˈmejɚ]

#34
Mid-Central R-Colored Tense Vowel (Stressed) /ɝ/

Position	Word	Transcription
Initial	irk	[ˈɝk]
Medial	turn	[ˈtɝn]
Final	purr	[ˈpɝ]

#35
High Back Tense Rounded Vowel /u/

Note: /u/ rarely occurs in initial position in SAE, such as in "oops."

Position	Word	Transcription
Medial	boom	[ˈbum]
Final	chew	[ˈtʃu]

#36
High Back Lax Rounded Vowel /ʊ/

Does not occur in initial or final positions of words in SAE.

Position	Word	Transcription
Medial	hook	[hʊk]
	butcher	[ˈbʊtʃɚ]

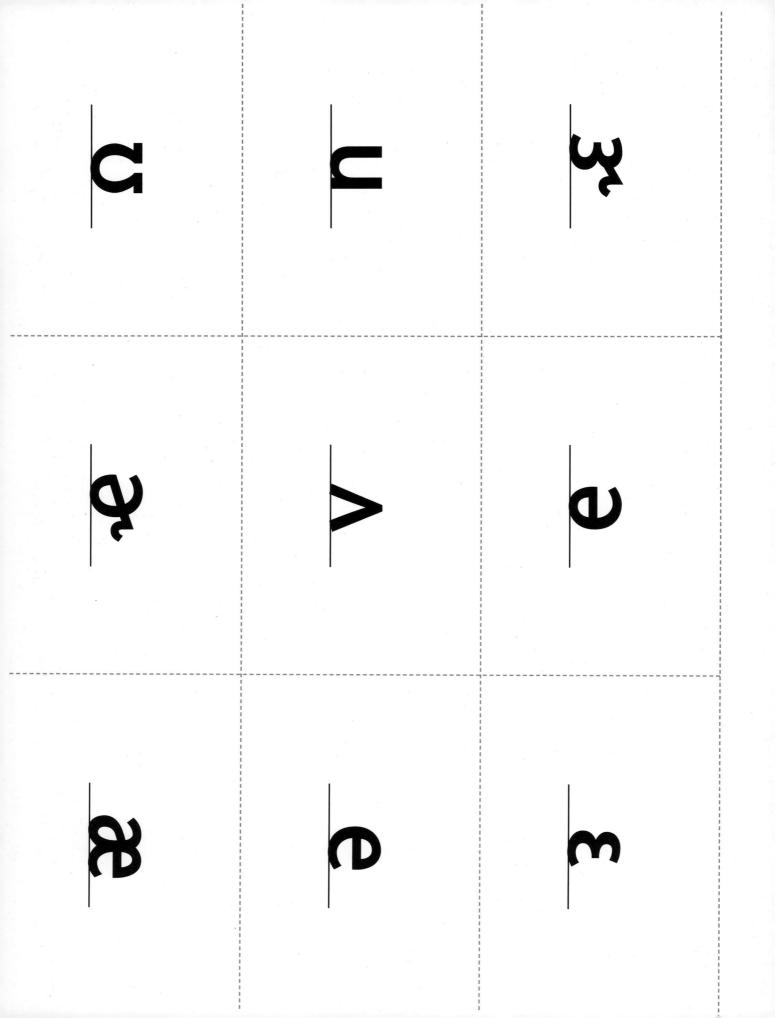

#37
Mid-Back Tense Rounded Vowel /o/

Initial   open   [opɪn]

Medial   pole   [pol]

Final   sew   [so]

#38
Low Mid-Back Lax Rounded Vowel /ɔ/

Initial   ostrich   [ɔstrɪtʃ]

Medial   dawn   [dɔn]

Final   thaw   [θɔ]

#39
Low Back Lax Unrounded Vowel /ɑ/

Initial   encore   [ɑnkor]

Medial   calm   [kɑlm]

Final   spa   [spɑ]

#40
Rising Low Front to High Front (Off-Glide) Diphthong /aɪ/

Initial   eye   [aɪ]

Medial   pine   [paɪn]

Final   sigh   [saɪ]

#41
Rising Low Front to High Back (Off-Glide) Diphthong /aʊ/

Initial   ouch   [aʊtʃ]

Medial   brown   [braʊn]

Final   vow   [vaʊ]

#42
Rising Mid-Back to High Front (Off-Glide) Diphthong /ɔɪ/

Initial   oil   [ɔɪl]

Medial   join   [dʒɔɪn]

Final   deploy   [dɪplɔɪ]

#43
High Front to High Back (On-Glide) Diphthong /ju/

Initial   use   [juz]

Medial   huge   [hjudʒ]

Final   pew   [pju]

juː

ɔɪ

aʊ

aɪ

p

c

o

#44
Vowel + r sequence /ɑr/

Initial	*ark*	[ˈɑrk]
Medial	*garden*	[ˈgɑrdɪn]
Final	*star*	[stɑr]

#45
Vowel + r sequence /or/

Initial	*oar*	[or]
Medial	*norm*	[ˈnorm]
Final	*your*	[jor]

#46
Vowel + r sequence /ir/

Initial	*era*	[ˈirʌ]
Medial	*fierce*	[ˈfirs]
Final	*here*	[ˈhir]

#47
Vowel + r sequence /ɛr/

Initial	*error*	[ˈɛrɚ]
Medial	*perish*	[ˈpɛrɪʃ]
Final	*stare*	[stɛr]

er

ir

or

ur